GONDOLIN PRESS

Ettore Gotti Tedeschi

Love God, make Money!

Principles of Divine Economics

gondolin press

LOVE GOD, MAKE MONEY – *Ettore Gotti Tedeschi*

Original title: *Amare Dio e fare soldi* (2014)

© Fede & Cultura (Italy)
www.fedecultura.com

Translator: Peter Waymel, revised by Ann Brown

© **gondolin press**
1331 Red Cedar Cir
80524 Fort Collins CO

www.gondolinpress.com
info@gondolinpress.com

2018 © Gondolin Institute LLC
Book ISBN 978-1-945658-06-8
eBook ISBN: 978-1-945658-07-5

First Italian edition: June 2014
First U.S. edition: June 2018

FOREWORD

If it is true (which it is) that man and not fate determines human history and man's present situation, and if it is true that the errors men make have negative consequences, then the modern world is our responsibility. We are, of course, responsible for the way democracy functions poorly, for the crisis in society and customs, and so on, but we are also responsible for the economic imbalances resulting from economic "science," which in fact is not a science, and from the difficulty we humans have in using economics as a means for the common good and managing it with a moral sense.

We realize that there is currently a crisis affecting man and the whole of civilization, but this crisis has existed for as long as man has existed, or more precisely, ever since man fell into sin. Not even the coming of Jesus Christ was enough to end it. Jesus showed us a path of individual salvation, of choosing between eternal economics and wholly earthly economics, but the awareness of evil and sin have faded over time and continue to do so today. The significance of human life, and the sense of what life and destiny are all about, are deteriorating faster than ever, and the quality and value of the civilization we are experiencing are waning.

We could say that our society is marked by absolute forms of humanism, liberalism, idealism, relativism, etc., the result of which is the disappearance of truth and certainty, and consequently the refusal to accept a moral law that is not generated by one's own free and independent conscience. What happens to economics without moral reference points that give it meaning? The economy becomes an instrument for dominating nature, with its autonomous laws (and morals).

Catholicism instead views the economy as a means to be used for the good of man, a means to be perfected as an instrument of salvation in the light of eternity, for those who use it and benefit from it. The principles and considerations that follow are expounded without any particular order and are sometimes repeated. They are the fruit of notes and reflections made over the years. Some of these reflections will cite the person who inspired them. They may be useful for reflection and individual formation for those who want to submit the instrument of economics to truth and the good, for the greater well-being of man.

PRINCIPLES

1

Materialism, which we shall frequently consider in this collection of principles and reflections on morals in economics, is the consequence of idealism. Idealism, the autonomous thought that excludes any other reality, is absolute pride. This allows, or even forces, the formation of our thought and will to be determined by our instincts, needs and passions, and so generates materialism which, as a philosophy and principle of action, necessitates the so-called pragmatism that leads us to seek only satisfaction, utility, efficiency and self-interest, without heeding our conscience.

Idealism exalts human intelligence, almost deifying it, with the logical consequence of man's absolute independence from any creator, leading to atheism and agnosticism. Idealistic morality is therefore a (pragmatic) form of morality that does not speak of a good to be reached or the purposes of actions and objects, and which too often confuses ends with means, bestowing moral autonomy on economics. Thus economics, no longer guided by moral norms based on recognized truths, manufactures truths for itself according to its needs, deciding that what is useful is also the good (and the only good), often renaming anarchy "economic liberty," or perhaps giving the name of "economic assistance" to what really is *dirigisme* or monopolistic state totalitarianism. This turns the economist into a type of high priest who possesses the keys to good and evil—which is going too far.

2

We must not be afraid to speak about morality in economics. Some would like economics to have its own moral "autonomy" so as to justify every action, or at least for economics not to have to submit to "various types of morals in the global world," but who's afraid of morals? Morals will never question the functioning of economic models, since the latter are a means, and morals are only concerned with the ends, that is, the meanings of our choices. Good and evil, which every man can commit, have an impact on society; therefore the degree of a nation's civilization, in any age, is measured by the use made of its instruments, including the economic ones. This is based on the notion of good and evil, not just on what is useful or efficient. Thus it is necessary to rediscover what is good and to have the courage to teach it unreservedly. If there were any doubt as to how to apply these moral norms, it would be enough to consider what criteria we apply to the creation of riches and the use we make of them. But one must think about this, and then he will see that the problem always concerns the necessary distinction between ends and means—a distinction not always clear to everyone. We therefore encourage all to examine this distinction as a priority.

3

We have the impression that man's moral progress in recent years has been inversely proportional to his progress in science and technology. Such knowledge in the hands of an immature man is the equivalent of a speeding car driven by a child. It is sufficient to observe the considerations made by the "learned" of this age regarding the meaning of life and regarding human nature, love, the family, procreation, and life and death. Would they have us believe that with the skills learned from science (biology, genetics, economics itself…) we can perfect human life, when they cannot even show us that they know what man is, what his end is, or what makes him happy or unhappy? How can we believe them?

4

If there were any doubt about man's "economic" obligations starting from the moment of Creation, it would suffice to read or reread the Old Testament carefully. The Book of Genesis tells how man was created and put in the Garden of Eden *ut operaretur*, "so that he would work it" (Gen 1:28); therefore he was not obliged to work only *after* being expelled from the earthly paradise, but even while he was still in it. This fact is not without deep significance, as God created man to love Him, to serve Him and to give Him glory; this is something closely related to work and gives it a divine purpose and most noble origin of which we should be proud: that of complementing Creation. Man's obligation to work did not begin with the Fall; however, now he must do so with fatigue: "In the sweat of your brow shall you eat your bread" (Gen 3:19). "Fallen" man must rise again through work. If this is clear to us, we cannot skip the step of reflecting on what this means in practice, today, whatever we do and wherever we are.

5

Ideologies are oriented to an end without evaluating the means, often confusing the means with the end: think of Marxism or Nazism. We must look for the meaning of acts that use the means, and always distinguish between the means and the ends.

6

Do you know how to produce wealth? This can be your mission for the benefit of your neighbor who does not know how, and it is therefore your duty to do so, but producing wealth is a means and not an end. Are you ignorant of how to produce wealth? Do what you know how to do as best you can, and do not envy those who know how to produce it. It is better to take advantage of the friendship of those who know how, being grateful towards them and helping them find meaning in their work.

7

Work becomes less burdensome when you consider it as a means rather than an end, and naturally if it *does* have an end. As a means, work must and can always be done better (in spite of failures and fatigue), and this can be done if the end becomes more ambitious.

8

The so-called alienation of man is not due to the obligation to work (which everyone can understand, as work is necessary for earning one's living), but is rather a reaction against a certain model of production which deprives man of other natural needs (real needs), without any explanation as to why. Alienation is the lack of clear meaning in one's work life. Does the economic "scientist" have any solution to this problem?

9

Learn from children the essence of work. Even they need to "work," and if they do so with dedication and satisfaction, they mature in a balanced way through play. Playing *is* their work. We are born "*ut operaretur.*"

10

Freedom from work and fatigue is a foolish presumption. Freedom is responsibility and above all the possibility of doing good, and in this world, good is achieved through labor.

11

Free time is not time to be wasted, but rather time to be used in a different way. Often it is more demanding than work time, but if it has meaning it can be more productive, satisfying and important than time dedicated to work.

12

In the past, *ars gratia artis* was the artist's and even the professional's motto. Today, as yesterday, art can produce wealth, but unlike yesterday when art consisted of producing masterpieces, today's masterpiece consists of knowing how to create a "market for art" and in selling the illusion that a work of art has been bought. There is a need for ethics in art, too.

13

Auri sacra fames (hunger for gold) is not necessarily greed, but arises from an understanding of the importance and necessity of money to do things consistently. Consistent things are done with ideas and money, but above all through the meaning of one's actions. Even good is often done with money; otherwise the Good Samaritan (who was a reviled merchant) would not have been able to help the well-known robbed man in the Gospel (who was ignored by the intellectual Levite); otherwise St. Martin would not have had a cloak to share with the poor man; otherwise the women in the Gospels would not have been able to provide for Jesus and His apostles from their means, and Joseph of Arimathea would not have had a tomb to offer Jesus. The rich man of the Gospels who does not enter the Kingdom of Heaven is not the one who produced wealth, but the one who made bad use of it (Dives) and ignored the poor man (Lazarus). Wealth cannot be considered a fault, nor can poverty (that which is endured, not willed) be considered merit. What confusion there still is today about these considerations!

14

Perhaps the rich young man of the Gospel failed to follow Christ not simply because he is too rich (although Christ's request should have encouraged him not a little...), but probably also because he did not have a vocation to apostolic life as an "apostle": perhaps he had a vocation to married life and did not find it within himself to abandon this choice. Perhaps, but as this parable is often used wrongly, it is good to clarify that wealth in itself is not, cannot be, and must not be an obstacle to holiness.

15

A true sacrilege that must be discussed in addition to the usual unjust distribution of wealth, is the absurd mystification of the value of wealth itself (well-produced and used well), as, moreover, its destruction is a waste, perpetrated by individuals as well as governments.

16

Wealth, like culture, health, physical strength, and even beauty, is a great means. What counts is the use one makes of it. Think of "culture," so vaunted today: is not using it badly, as often happens, a flaunting of badly-managed wealth?

17

Although I appreciate many results of its work, I am not sure I love philanthropy: all too often it performs charity without love, out of fear of the poor, to make oneself loved and appreciated.

18

To paraphrase the French writer and essayist Montaigne (1533-1592) when he says: "It is more difficult to earn money than to save it," today I would say it is more difficult to save it. Furthermore I would say it is easier today to earn it well than to spend it well.

19

The Jewish writer Kafka, who was born in Prague in 1883 and died in Vienna in 1924, had an extraordinary intuition for perceiving and recognizing that intellectual work could distance man from the human community, while "manual" work could bring him closer to his peers. This is true, but intellectual work with a good end can be even better.

20

The Swiss Huguenot philosopher Rousseau (1712-1788) was right when he said that it is difficult to think nobly when one only thinks of earning a living. This is true, but not "when one is forced" to do so out of a sense of responsibility, but rather when one "thinks only of that"...

21

It is difficult to contradict St. Paul's words: "If any man will not work, neither let him eat." It is easy to contradict the French philosopher Voltaire (1694-1788) who wrote that "the only way to make life bearable is to work without reasoning" (*Candide*).

22

The truly poor man is a fortunate rich man because he is wise (I do not remember who said this). The Spanish mystic St. Teresa of Ávila (1515-1582) also said that the truly poor man is the one who makes no noise.

23

That poverty can exist in an economic system of abundance is a fact linked to what relative poverty means, but above all to the fixed costs (technological and political) of a civilization of well-being (from condo fees, to waste tax, to ever-looming taxes). For that matter, in a democracy, the high cost of a State is above all the fixed and untouchable costs of ignoring the citizens' rights to decide for themselves the minimum costs they must pay.

24

Where human work is not inspired by "Catholic culture," either one lives fatalistically (Hinduism), detached from everything (Buddhism), miserably (Animism), restraining one's inner capacities and not trusting in individual merits (Islam), anxiously craving success as a blessing from God (Protestantism), or making success the goal and working with only human and very earthly motives: health, beauty, or consumption (secularism).

25

Capitalism as the economic system opposed by the German political economist Marx (1818-1883) did not originate in a Catholic spirit, but was produced by the Protestant heresy (which invited people to sin as much as they wished provided that they deeply repented); it was produced by human actions unconcerned with avoiding personal sin, trying to do everything well, or doing good with each act. It is good to remember that the religion opposed and fought by Marx was in the end a religion deformed by heresy.

26

If the earth belonged to everyone and all private property were forbidden, the earth would not be anyone's in practice, and no one would care for it as it should be cared for; no one would value or protect it. Private property, a sacred principle that cannot be disregarded, is a way of protecting the earth, not the opposite. The opposite occurs when this principle is abused; hence abuses rather than principles should be punished!

27

Free trade of goods permits us to enjoy other people's products and at the same time develop (excluding "exploitation") other economies with competitive and thus effective models. This promotes general global well-being and therefore becomes a logical and natural form of solidarity. Protectionism, however, is foolish and counterproductive selfishness for those who apply it, not just for those who suffer from it. Free trade is moral if it is engaged in under political systems in which all are truly free, while protectionism is more mistaken than immoral.

28

Economic competition is the best way to ensure two types of freedom: freedom of choice among the various options available, and freedom to find the best price in all sectors, especially for those less well-off. Competition, as an economic principle, is just.

29

The greatest drama of recent times, which has produced poverty and irreversible economic imbalances, has been to believe that the specter of poverty is the consequence of population growth. It was like imposing the end of the free market and the absolute protection of one's own status. Natural and economic laws have shown this mistake and its consequences, yet the prophets of error seem to be the only ones reaping advantages for themselves; although they caused the errors, they now continue to produce "remedies" with the same spirit and "prophetic vision."

30

In economics the error is often not so much attachment to money through greed, but is rather linked to fear, mistrust and lack of a sense of the supernatural: for example, avarice cannot be a vice of the greedy. The French Doctor of the Church, St. Bernard (1091-1153), said that avarice is living in continual misery for fear of misery. The cause of this fear is the lack of a certain virtue which faith would provide; it is the absence of real trust in oneself, which comes from a life founded on trust in Divine Providence.

31

It is a curious fact that some people hate and criticize progress (which is manifestly good) and would love to turn back the clock (which they would consider a good thing): these people consider man a beast dangerous to nature, which must be protected from human action. This reminds me of the twelfth-century Catharist heresy.

32

Private property is legitimate and indispensable; the problem is that if you don't know how to justify it, it will not necessarily remain in the same hands. All in all, this can be a good thing.

33

The fall of the so-called *élite* is not so much connected to the corruption of customs as to the fact that they never even dreamed of building responsibly on the talents they had available.

34

Many years ago I was struck when I read a phrase by the English philosopher Francis Bacon (1561-1626) which I quote from memory: "Wealth is a good servant, but the worst of lovers…"

35

The Irish writer Swift (1667-1745) wrote an ironic essay on wealth (an essay definitely not loved by Protestants, who consider wealth a sign of God's blessing), which is worth remembering here: "If God had considered wealth a truly precious gift, He would certainly not have granted it to so many imbeciles."

36

It is odd how in conflicting discussions between science and faith, many so-called scientists show an unmitigated hatred of religion, which they claim limits and hinders the advantages "their" science could offer humanity, without demonstrating exactly how this is so. One could say that "their" science, comprised more of promises than of relevant experiences, competes against religion and faith's promises. Since one expects results and not vague promises from science, and since one expects demonstrable explanations and not inexplicable theories (such as evolutionism), science is at a loss before the promises of religion and becomes its harshest enemy instead of ignoring it as one might expect it to do.

37

There is little doubt that Christian asceticism (found in Benedictine monasteries, for example) had a fundamental role in the development of capitalism, showing the usefulness of reinvesting the wealth it produced to improve and develop useful tools for man. There are doubts, however, that the same asceticism could have stimulated and appreciated so-called consumerism. Today, in our world where rich and poor countries and people co-exist without borders, it would be difficult to satisfy the material needs of the poorest if consumers do not multiply in the richest countries. Paradoxically, the consumerism of rich countries enables low-cost production in poor countries. This is based on the economic concept of "volume" and on the consequent economy of scale: if I produce (and someone consumes) one billion (of a product, food, medicine, garment...) versus a million, obviously the production cost will be different (it will be lower), benefiting those with low or even zero purchasing power. Those who make this possible are those who have higher purchasing power—in other words, the accursed "consumers."

38

What role does human work have within the meaning of life? Industriousness is not the first virtue, and work in and of itself does not instill joy or give life meaning (as Giambattista Torellò wrote in *From the Walls of Jericho*). What is more, we discover that the great economic revolutions are creations of the spirit and not of hunger. We also know that idolizing work deprives man of his best qualities. Great thinkers from many different backgrounds have warned us of this "temptation" to exaggerate the importance of work in the life of man (the idolatry of work) as opposed to the importance of knowledge, wisdom and passion for the truth. The French Jewish writer Simone Weil, a cultural Christian though never baptized, wrote that one could be part of the élite that governs the world and not have the faintest idea of his destiny.

Let us reflect: how true is it for us who study in order to work, eat to return to work, rest to be able to work, even marry to be able to work better... that this is all just a vicious circle? Was it perhaps to this that Voltaire referred (see Principle 21) when he wrote that work is the means of sparing man the fatigue (and privilege) of thinking? Does work, praised to the skies like this, have something demonic about it? Of course not, but man must consider work only as a means to an end, and to do this he must place it within a scheme of life that contemplates other things—the spirit, for example—otherwise he will end up with a tremendous imbalance. As man is both body and soul, so must his actions be coherent and consistent: work and spirit. Thus work itself becomes contemplation, and in this way one

ennobles and values it. St. Josemaría Escrivá (1902-1975), the founder
of Opus Dei, wrote: "Whoever wants to live his own faith with
perfection and practice the apostolate according to the spirit of Opus
Dei must sanctify himself with his profession, sanctify his profession
and sanctify others with his profession." *(Conversations* no. 70) Thus
we will contemplate the world with affection and gratitude, not with
greed, envy, selfishness and utilitarianism.

39

When I was young, children were taught the sacredness of saving,
a fundamental virtue in the period of economic reconstruction in the
decade following the war. A ritual I remember was depositing my little
coins monthly in a metal box (the key to which I did not have); this
key was kept at a bank (called a "savings bank," in fact). Then I moved
up to a ceramic piggy bank, which was to be broken when some
special occasion was coming up and I wanted to spend the money
saved. The piggy bank has progressively disappeared, along with the
habit of saving, and spending has become a virtue, money having
become something trifling to use immediately. Some exult over this,
not only the shopkeepers but also the moralists who want to see
people totally detached from money, a dangerous object of affection
and consequent loss of the sense of the supernatural since money
incites either miserliness or spendthrift ways. But… away with these
ideas! Saving must be taught again; it should be seen as a human
means so that it is not transformed into an occasion of sin. Instead,
one must teach generosity, which gives money a supernatural
meaning.

40

Faith in so-called progress that scientific man guarantees with
science, know-how and technology has really and truly become a
superstition, because it excludes any other "faith" which takes into
account the limits of scientific knowledge and distinguishes such
knowledge from the meaning (and birth) of life itself in its approach.
As the German existentialist philosopher Karl Jaspers (1883-1969)
reminds us, utopias are thinking that we have understood everything

and know it all; that we can solve every problem and difficulty; that we can improve existence with economic well-being, imposing democracy as an effective way of freedom, etc.… These considerations are from 1931, and today Jaspers would update them in desperation. What has to happen so that disillusioned man can re-examine his faith in these utopias?

41

I maintain that neither Jews nor Protestants still believe that (economic) success equals the blessing of God; otherwise they would have to recognize that often God blesses not them but some poor idiot. However, if we sought to deepen the meaning of success for each one of us, we would discover that this lies in the education we have had in a context of dominant values at a certain moment. Note well, it is the almost mathematical measurability of success (money, power, status symbols…) that makes it lack credibility. Virtues are not measured, intelligence itself is not measured, and neither are knowledge and wisdom. Virtues are measured by the results they produce, it is true, but they are not quantifiable (except by standards which not everyone shares, such as number of children, number of students taught, number of converts, etc.).

We must therefore prepare ourselves to face the challenges of competition for a success whose criteria are established by prevailing standards, otherwise we risk wasting time and losing effectiveness. Take note, the search for and achievement of success is hardly an evil in itself. Man must be prepared to detach himself from success and accept the possible lack thereof should that happen; he must know that a lack of success becomes success for a discerning person if he learns from it. What counts, as in everything, is how one goes forward and for what reason: if one has the gift and ability to find success in a certain field, it is good and useful to do so, as that "field" is enriched when one gives it a sense of the divine and supernatural. The parable of the talents shows us clearly that God does not look down on esteeming one's own abilities, but rather expects it.

42

Undoubtedly the end justifies the means (in economics as in other disciplines); if the ends did not justify them, how and why would such means have been chosen? The problem that perhaps inappropriately reminds us of the Florentine political writer Machiavelli (1469-1527) is: *which* ends justify *which* means? A "good" end cannot be justified by "bad" means. A good end which can only be reached by bad means must not be pursued or, in my opinion, the means must be reconsidered strategically based on this premise: there are no good ends that can be reached only by bad means, but there are men who do not know how to find good means, so we return to the theme of personal responsibility and the need for formation.

43

There is (in economics, for example) no instrument ethical in itself, but there are men who by their behavior render any legitimate instrument ethical. If this were not the case, how many people with unethical objectives would make so-called ethical instruments their own in order to do evil? I do not therefore believe in an "ethical bank," "ethical capital" or "ethical organizations" in themselves. What counts and guarantees their "ethicalness" are the ethics of those in charge, and that the established ends, results and means are all carefully checked.

44

How can someone be a working man in his location and sector while at the same time being a saver and consumer in the global context? The saver and consumer in him can destroy his work when he invests his savings elsewhere and purchases foreign goods, consequently destroying his own savings and consumption—this man who is working in a non-competitive area or sector to produce products which can be sold and attract savings, and this happens in the Western world when an economy has (immorally) been under state protection for too long.

45

What will happen with the transfer of wealth (savings, investments and consumption) to the so-called emerging producer states (such as China and India)? Apart from wealth, will the values and culture of "Western" countries be transferred to them, or will these newly-rich emerging countries transfer their values and culture to us (which would be a repudiation of our roots)?

46

As imposed multiculturalism (the co-existence of various cultures) is engendering cultural relativism (a fact welcomed by almost everyone), multi-economics (the co-existence of several types of economies) is instead causing a form of technocratic, undemocratic absolutism in supra-national organizations created to regulate globalization. One could say that economics, unlike culture, fears "economic relativism" whereby each person can interpret economic laws as he wishes, which creates incompatible and competing economic models. National governments, which can now (because they are forced to) formulate laws which are homogenous among states (and not necessarily in line with the wishes of the different populations), are at the same time unable to guarantee order and security, unable to guarantee a competitive market with all its benefits and free from the opposition of lobbies, unable to avoid justifying camouflaged public interventions, unable to give individuals choice when it comes to school education, etc. They are highly incapable, yet ever more expensive, and then there are supra-national governments. Well, who pays for these supra-national governments? Who elects them, who legitimizes them and who corrects them? One would answer: national governments. Fine, but in exchange for what: the survival and growth of these national governments?

47

I am more and more convinced that the so-called moralization of economics can occur only if those who decide on economic matters are made to feel some responsibility for it, but what responsibility?

About what? How can people be made to feel responsible? With courses on morals? With company balance sheets? With papal encyclicals? Max Weber, the German sociologist (1864-1920), distinguished between ethics of responsibility and ethics of conviction, but how can responsibility for one's actions be guaranteed if one is not fully convicted by this responsibility? Can this conviction disregard an absolute value? Experience says no: those with convictions and the desire and know-how to realize them are those able to change the world.

48

If it is true (as it is) that behavior influences thought, then if thought is not strong enough to determine behavior, then no behavior is more "influential" than economic behavior. Working, producing, investing, spending, learning and competing are necessary behaviors, and refusing to engage in them means excluding oneself from the world. What is more, in the (economic) world, Gresham's famous Law is still in force (named after Elizabeth I's financial adviser, 1519-1579), which states that bad money drives out good. Translated in another way, one could say that "bad" behavior drives out good, becoming a competitive reference point. I would ask that we reflect on how in recent times economic power has prevailed over political power (modifying laws) and over religious power (actively seeking to relativize faith and adapt norms to the market), and how much it has changed the behavior (and the thoughts) of man. Must we reconquer the economy in order to reclaim man? By showing that morals in economics produce more positive effects and improve competitive advantages? Yes, but do we really believe that? And are we still capable of doing this?

49

Economic power consists of imposing as many needs and conditions (price, earnings, purchasing power, labor intensity, work training, time given over to other activities, other values etc.) as necessary. Not accepting these impositions means ignoring a need, but can you ignore many needs without leaving this world? One economic law dictates that one is excluded if one does not participate. It is therefore true that we must learn to remain *in* the world without becoming…. too much *of* the world. That means satisfying our needs without satisfying ourselves, which means accepting conditions without submitting to them.

50

True detachment from goods that we legitimately have at our disposal, whether they be money, objects, houses, furniture, clothing or jewelry, is in reality only detachment from ourselves, that is, from our own less noble inclinations and weaknesses. Our detachment serves to make way for other truer and nobler values, such as contemplation, simplicity, humility and practicality, which enrich man more fully. Detachment from goods does not mean not having them or not using them, but means actually "using" them, or in other words, considering them as a means according to one's state and necessity, not worshipping them or considering them ends in themselves.

One of many things we missed out on in religious education, when they aimed to give us "norms suited to the times," was detachment. Since mortification is the best example of detachment (having something, having the possibility to have it and enjoy it, but doing without it), the well-known but neglected Friday abstinence from meat was a simple, continual, easy and educational form of "painless" mortification, teaching us to train our egos. This Friday offering also reminded us of Jesus' Passion. In losing this habit we have also lost an important practice of motivated sacrifice. Let us not then complain about dechristianization…

51

Competition can (I repeat, *can*) become a means of balance and justice when it can be transformed into a true natural limit to economic power, allowing us to choose. Note well: not only to choose work or goods, but above all to choose conditions that satisfy our needs…. Competition, carried out according to licit, transparent and effective criteria, is fair and can be ethical.

52

Wealth does not necessarily express power. It is the *investment* of wealth that determines power, and today this capacity is more separate from the availability of wealth than ever. Those who manage wealth (whether company managers or investment fund managers), not the shareholders, have the real responsibility for this economic power. Here too, there is competition (regarding confidence and its results) which safeguards the good use of this power. Competition represents a careful, permanent form of "checks and balances" on the exercise of economic power.

53

It is strange how today no philosophical current or political party supports the ethics of mortification of needs or the necessity of detachment from things. Apparently everyone thinks that justice and equity mean having goods, not going without them. Catholic morality still teaches detachment from things, although with greater prudence, as does Buddhist morality (and also Islamic morality, but in a very different way, as detachment is imposed by the Koran and not left to individual freedom). From a completely different ideological viewpoint, the ecological movement also thinks this way, preaching a reshaping of progress for the good of the planet and, consequently, for man. The Catholic, on the other hand, holds that only with greater (technological) progress can one improve the environment (which, by the way, is much less damaged than ecologists say it is). Oddly, but not as a contradiction, today the Catholic finds himself defending progress by speaking more about detachment from goods through using them in a way that sanctifies, rather than doing without them.

54

For once, I must quote with approval the English economist J.M. Keynes (1883-1946): "Economics does not create civilization, but the possibility of civilization." I agree with this thought, but I must correct it. It is obvious that economics cannot create a civilization. Economics is an instrument, a means at the disposal of a type of civilization that shows the extent of its development by the use it makes of economic instruments. But what determines this "elevatedness" of civilization is the underlying cultural level that inspires it, and this cultural level, in judging what is good and evil, is based on morals. The quality of a civilization, apart from the means available to it, depends on the use of economic instruments. Economics at the service of man is true civilization. Man as the instrument of production and consumption, in service to the economy, is not true civilization, but its cemetery.

At times economists (like Marx) have had—and some still have today—the temptation to explain to us what good is and what it does, competing with and even taking the place of the philosopher, theologian or priest. As J.B. Say, French economist (1736-1832) who lived through the French Revolution and the Napoleonic era, wrote: "The best moral lessons one can give a people are political economics lessons." Referring to moral problems (which Marx contested as bourgeois ethics), Say might have been right had he understood that political economics was a mere means by which all can use their abilities to produce benefits for everyone, and consequently for themselves as well, instead of stating that individual selfishness produces collective advantages. Is there a society in the world where a rich, privileged (and exploitative) few co-exist with all the others being poor (and exploited)? Perhaps in an economic system linked to only one natural resource (petroleum, for example) where a few rich people enjoy their privileged wealth thanks to... money and foreign purchases, or perhaps in a (temporarily) Communist regime, which history shows us cannot be sustained in the long run. The fact is that wealth can only be sustained if it is spread around, not out of fear of revolution but for purely economic reasons. Wealth is maintained by its continual creation and growth, implying that all can enjoy it freely, freely earning and therefore freely consuming.

55

What moral obligation do we have in regard to economics? The fulfillment of our own duties. But what duties do Catholics have in economics? If the answer were to be simplified as far as possible, I would say that these duties are to work and produce as best one can, respecting the dignity of the person, one's own dignity as well as that of his neighbor. Respecting one's own dignity means giving the correct significance to one's own work (how much, under what conditions, for what end); respecting that of others means justice and charity toward them.

56

Does economic well-being produce greater happiness? St. Augustine (354-430) suggested asking God *ora beatam vitam*, asking Him for a happy life now. The origin of philosophy lies in man's desire to be happy, which is why he wishes to know himself, understand what he is and why, and know what he therefore needs. Since man no longer lives in an earthly paradise, and thus has to work to live, the problem of happiness needs an organizational solution, translating principles (such as the Commandments) into practical, practicable virtues.

What does working virtuously mean? It means giving the best of oneself according to one's capacities, talents, conditions, responsibilities, etc. In practice it means doing one's best, which produces results leading to economic well-being. Conclusion: if the economic well-being produced is the result of (certain) virtues we practice, it certainly contributes to greater happiness, as does the practice of all other virtues. The more complex question is whether happiness is truly the most essential thing in human life. St. Josemaría Escrivá was certain that if a man acted as a child of God, he could be happy on this earth while at the same time aspiring to eternal life.

57

We believe, differently from other "visions of life," or more precisely, differently from other "visionaries" of life, that human life is shaped by a goal. Thus the coherence of life produces the balance that we call happiness. This is true for the economic aspect just as for any other. Working and producing wealth and well-being are a means, an instrument for doing something else, something more important. This more important "something else" is the goal that gives meaning to work, to the effort and sacrifices made, to the wealth produced, to life's end. Morality is the "science" that teaches man the meaning of life and the scope of his actions. Without this, these actions have only a relative and often ineffective meaning.

58

The Beatitudes show us privations and suffering (poverty, need, detachment…) as means of sanctification. However, privation and suffering are not only physical or emotional, but also moral when man questions the meaning of life and of his actions and deprives himself of many pleasures he considers dangerous or wrong. For whoever ponders the meaning of life, failure is something totally different than failure seen by those who only consider success or lack thereof. For the Catholic, failure is not finding the meaning of his own life.

59

We can truly be God's "bankers." St. Augustine wrote: "If virtue leads us to a happy life, I dare to affirm that virtue is nothing other than supreme love of God." In Christian tradition the virtue *par excellence* is charity, which is love of God, and through this love, it is love towards one's neighbor and oneself. What are the obligations of charity? St. Augustine explained that when we love, whatever we do is good, but there is no real charity without renunciation (of something), because often God shows mercy toward those in need through us and our actions. We are therefore God's intermediaries, almost like God's "bankers," who freely dispense (as intermediaries) help on His behalf. Real justice is crowned with charity, much more than with judicial justice.

60

What would sin be in the field of economics? As economics is an instrument and a means (and not a very scientific one at that), sin does not lie in economics but in the use one makes of it. It is subjective, linked to individual choice and personal responsibility. The more an economic instrument makes progress, the more everyone notices how much better off people are, but they fail to notice how those who have responsibility and power could help others to be even better off by not considering man a means of production, savings, or consumption, or a means of paying taxes to those who govern badly, etc. Sometimes—far too often, in fact—when people forget what the conditions are for bringing about economic well-being, they risk rendering their best intentions and actions futile.

61

Economic "science" views man as the object of the satisfaction he is destined for, and believes his success to be the result of this satisfaction, because it judges man by the external. This is good. Moral "science" considers human (economic) actions from the viewpoint of man's interior, according to the meaning he gives them and the way he carries them out. I believe that economic science has need of moral science, otherwise it remains too external to man and concerns itself solely with the visible aspects of his actions. Without a moral impulse or reflection, in dealing with economics one cannot consider interior facets which are fundamental to human life, such as one's perception of good and evil, love and hate, motivation or lack thereof, resentment and gratitude, truth and falsehood, a sense of duty, etc. Without understanding these points it is difficult, if not impossible, to understand, explain and evaluate human actions. One can manage to make a "good confession" with a good priest without reasoning or psychoanalysis.

In conclusion, economic science, which is concerned with providing for man's material needs, is not enough to "satisfy" man. No one claims this of this field, it is true, but those who study it must pay attention to the certainties it does have, so that it can succeed at least some of the time. Economic science only deals with theories of man's economic behavior, and not with his interior life, and so cannot tell us what man truly needs. Morality should be based on economic science in order to make appropriate moral judgments about human actions, as it does not always provide the economic, social and cultural factors that explain human actions. If necessary, (those studying or formulating) moral laws must be able to comprehend needs and satisfactions in order to correct them.

62

For many centuries, the Catholic moralist has played an often authoritarian and sometimes even exaggerated educational role (for example, having little trust that men could lead virtuous lives…). Later on the Catholic moralist had an exaggerated attitude of openness to the contemporary world, abdicating his role of teacher and even confusing the very role of morality or treating it as inferior compared to the ever-evolving human sciences, accepting a morality "suited to the times," that is, in tune with fashion. In economic matters the various currents of thought which have influenced moral perspectives have been mercantilism, the cult of the body, utilitarianism, Marxism….

Today, models of global competition create dominant opinions in moral matters as well (for example, relativism), but morality has the duty to remind people of the principles for judging social and economic phenomena, not for discussing their functions (as they are neutral instruments in themselves). The economy functions according to rules and market laws, not according to moral laws. Morals only serve to give meaning to economic actions, to direct them toward the good and the true, and must enlighten man regarding his dignity as a person and remind him of his spiritual duties toward God and neighbor. It is the individual, enlightened by conscience and mature in spirit (and not only learned in science), who must choose. Thus moral reasoning must not be subject to cultural or scientific fashion but must remain universal in time and space; it must be steadfast through the varying historical periods and evolutions in science itself. Moral reasoning must not be swayed by the dialectic arrogance of scientists, economists or intellectuals who are against morals. A moralist who can be intimidated and looks for compromises should be dismissed….

63

I want to remind you of what Carl Gustav Jung (1875-1961, the Swiss psychiatrist and opponent of Freudian psychoanalysis) said, referring to science: "One can say that economic science is not a perfect instrument (alas, it really is not); however, it is indispensable for progress. It does nothing but harm if it is viewed as an end in itself…" Well-said. In fact, economic science (as any other science) is made to serve, but if it imposes the application of its own "absolute" knowledge to establish what is good or bad (in human behavior) and how man must behave, it becomes a dictator instead of serving.

64

Often we see science pitted against morality; we hear that morality is theoretical and relative, based on religious principles that are always changing, often useless or even harmful if applied. Science, instead, is practical and universal, and produces real perceptible results of value to mankind.

First of all, morality is practical and not theoretical, because it concerns behavior and produces actions. If anything, it is science that is theoretical, while technology—the application of science—is practical. We could therefore say that morality can be better compared to technology than to science, and that morality is the "technology" of human behavior. In economic actions, morality raises questions about the consequences of applying economic laws, and about the resulting human behavior, and gives guidelines.

65

While economics does not concern the personal attitudes and intentions of those who apply it, morality is concerned precisely with the attitude and intentions of those who perform economic actions. Thus a person can be a great economist, banker, financier, or manager while being dishonest (with predictable consequences). In the same way, an honest person can be a modest banker, financier or manager (with equally predictable consequences). Morality concerns people and their actions, not their talents. Technology concerns man's technical capacities and results, and not the meaning he gives them. While technology gives one the ability to accomplish something, but does not necessarily force him to do so, morality motivates one to do something, if it is good, and to do it well. Benedictine monasteries, a type of Silicon Valley, were founded on morality and technology, *ora et labora*, and produced science, technology, knowledge, wealth and holiness….

66

I believe that the main problem in the progressively greater distance between moral vision and the application of economic science probably lies in the contrast between the development of economics and science and the development of man's spiritual maturity. This, as Pope John Paul II recalled in *Laborem Exercens*, has led to an imbalance of priorities between objective work and subjective work, that is, between economic laws and the (consequent) condition of man. Man is now certainly better off thanks to economic progress, but is he able to be a man, a child of God? Yes, of course, whoever wants to can do this, but only with great effort. It is puzzling how well-off contemporary man must toil far more than before to be a man of moral behavior. But I add, if I may: which is truly "real" behavior?

67

One could say that morality is human science *par excellence*; it is concerned with man's behavior. Jesus was the example of human behavior *par excellence*. In conformity with His humanity He recognized and revealed "the original man of Creation" both in the rich Zacchaeus and in the thief on the cross. Either a modern Zacchaeus or a modern thief (penitent, of course) can perfectly sanctify himself in everyday life. Of course, to do so, one must have a plan of life and be prepared to fight not a little…

68

The economic manual *par excellence* is the Sermon on the Mount (the Beatitudes), which I will not comment on here, but I remind you that the Our Father is an essential "appendix" to this, from which we learn to ask, like children, how to apply this manual's instructions.

69

It is worth reflecting on a consideration made by St. Francis de Sales (1567-1622) on morality in economics, compared with one by St. Josemaría Escrivá (1902-1975). St. Francis invites us to sanctify ourselves in the world *despite* the difficulties of so doing, while St. Josemaría invites us and teaches us to do this right *amidst* the difficulties of the world, to transform the world from within without becoming worldly.

70

Let us consider Protestant economic ethics. Protestants deny the possibility of sanctifying ourselves through economic activities (thanks to our nature, which they hold is corrupted by original sin), and invite us to act as if "there were no God," and even to sin in order to repent afterwards. This way of thinking should explain success in business, when the businessman doesn't worry too much about whether an action is good or evil, and should explain the hurried way the Protestant world makes decisions. Does this also explain why capitalist economic behavior has become so nonchalant and risky? I believe so.

71

After the Second Vatican Council, the consequent opening to the modern world, which implied freedom of conscience, ecumenism, pluralism, dialogue... led to a series of excesses: an excessive love of novelty, variety, and relativity; an excessive "allergy" to tradition; and an excessively subjective conscience with its consequent overly-wide opening towards the modern, and to the call to reforming everything in some way in moral matters, in the "light" of the (dominant) Marxist, Freudian, Nietzschean, Darwinian, Rousseauian, etc. thought.

Thanks to these excesses, Christian morality is subjected to public opinion and above all to currents of thought that before were criticized or denied: liberalism, socialism, positivism, idealism, existentialism, etc. With a good number of the clergy lacking in knowledge and training and (as we discovered afterwards) even with little faith or vocation, the opening to the world signified for many a moral surrender. Thus, in a very short space of time we were transformed from a Church with teaching authority into a Church with little credibility, a Church even viewed with distrust; a Church that no longer has much to offer, above all in the moral sphere. Her teachings are now reduced to human morals based solely on human and not on supernatural values, no longer influenced by a desire for God.

Now, especially in terms of economic morality, the problem has become more serious thanks to the process of naturalization, which is the reduction of human actions according to a natural order in which science (economic science being one example) dominates, affirming its principles as the only ones which lead to man's true good and well-being, where (in economics) only what is useful is good. There is no more faith, hope or charity, which should inspire individual behavior in man when he carries out economic laws which, being means, should necessarily have an end. If the end is merely material well-being, we should no longer wonder, as I said above, as the process of de-christianization continues.

72

In today's global world, poverty or wealth has a more relative conceptual meaning than in the past, a meaning linked to the times of acquisition. The so-called rich person has a temporal advantage in being able to enjoy the advantages of progress. The poor man has not yet reached this point, but it is only a question of time, if some "philosopher" or politician does not interrupt the mechanism through which he is destined to get there. In a free system, in the current technological situation and with current market logic, well-being for all is a question of time and… of [overcoming] obstacles. What people in our so-called Western, rich civilization classify as "unsatisfied needs" are no longer basic bodily necessities, as in other parts of the planet; they are the effect of comparison with others who have already satisfied such needs.

73

The so-called wealthy world has become so primarily due to various cultural factors rather than to the available resources. What was available to them was only the capacity to freely use knowledge. The wealthy world is not only rich because it *possesses* technological knowledge; it has technical know-how because it is free to develop such knowledge. This gift of knowledge is available to the so-called "poor" world, which will be able to share in that progress more rapidly, with lower costs and greater advantages [than the "rich world" did]. But for this to happen, no political obstacles must be put in the way, either in the "rich" world or in the "poor" world.

74

No doubt, "progress" produces infinite advantages and deprives us of other advantages that are just as important. Progress, however, is not "democratic," and the individual cannot vote in a (generic) referendum against progress, nor can he decide to distance himself from it. He must learn to co-exist, adapt, make use of advantages and resolve problems. Success depends on governments' abilities to help populations do this. I prefer not to comment on "how" they have too often done this and continue to do so.

75

Not only material well-being but also man's physical well-being, and even world peace, depend on progress. Progress can improve a civilization by improving the available instruments, the use of which alone reflects that civilization's level of development. If we cannot agree on the ethics of the use of these instruments, it is unthinkable that progress can produce a better natural order; instead, it will produce conflicts between those who wish to ignore the morality of acts, and those who cannot do so.

76

An economic system in a mature and wise civilization (as wise as it can be) is the fruit as much of the intellectual and moral capacities of those in charge, as it is of the circumstances. In practice it is the combination of the economic man's abilities and instincts, with those of the persons in government positions. The problem has always been reconciling human selfishness (which drives the economy) with public interest. According to Jeremy Bentham, the English economist (1748-1832), every law that limits (economic) freedom is a violation of liberty, while according to Marx, the German political economist (1818-1883), the word *businessman* is tantamount to the word *wrongdoer*. In reality, no serious academic has ever believed in the natural goodness of man, and therefore in the non-necessity of laws regulating his actions, just as no sane academic has ever believed that strong government control is the way a state creates well-being. In reality the individual has a capacity for (more or less enlightened) rational action which some government institutions, in some contexts, manage to appreciate, but others use this ability badly by wasting resources, time, and human capacities, sometimes even creating victims. It is correct to render to Caesar what is Caesar's, but what and how much is Caesar's, and why?

77

In times past, some—the eighteenth-century rationalists, for example (and some still today)—maintained that it is necessary to establish moral rules of behavior adapted to human nature to regulate the mechanisms governing the economic world, and they proceeded to do so, forgetting that "human nature," which they believe they know, is easily adaptable to the moral norms they wish to impose. It sounds simple, but with the persistent confusion between knowing economic laws and thinking one knows human nature…

78

Normally, most people try to adapt their actions to respect the aspirations and actions of others, which necessarily implies less efficient individual behavior, from an egotistical point of view. At least, thanks to our Christian roots, this is what our ethics should be toward others, toward minorities, with the solidarity that leads us to accept these norms with discipline and resignation when they are applied by law, even unjustly.

If ,however, we put aside our usual habits and tried to evaluate the laws and norms which moderate our behavior, which should benefit others whose needs are different from ours, we would discover that most of them have no logical foundation; most are harmful and useless, and benefit those who govern rather than those who are governed. We have no choice but to submit ourselves to them, without the hope that they will change if the government changes. We have the impression that too many governments operate with the excuse of managing "moral" principles and needs and defend their bad work by attacking [admittedly immoral] individual selfishness.

79

The theme of equality/inequality is dear to me because it allows me to talk about the importance of individual merit. In a book I wrote in 2004 with Rino Cammilleri (*Denaro e Paradiso,* or *Money and Paradise*), I reflected that equality, imposed as a right, represents a disadvantage to the individual, while inequality is an advantage. First, when inequality is recognized, the individual immediately finds a higher goal to reach for and ways to improve himself. Secondly, only in diversity can one be better or worse than others. Is it sensible and useful to expect equal results from utopian equality? Aside from the true equality that exists only before God (and the Law…), I remind you that the real equality to be sought and defended is in opportunities and not in results. Once again, in the wisdom of the Sacred Scriptures we find an exhortation not to wish for or believe in equality, when these texts condemn envy (one of the seven deadly sins) as a passion that harms man (especially the weakest) and society itself. This is most true when equality is disguised as mandatory social justice.

80

If I had to choose only one example to defend capitalism, I would say that it enabled people to start families and procreate responsibly. Until it became useful and possible for businessmen to invest their own capital in productive activities, thus giving work to many farmers and unemployed people (called proletarians, but in reality workers and stable income earners), those who wanted to start families and have children had to just be really lucky (as in already owning land and a house) or sacrifice much more, working the land for others in a hand-to-mouth existence.

81

The contemporary Austrian economist F.A. Hayek (in *The Free Society*) writes that "a defense of democracy presupposes that a minority opinion can become a majority opinion." This is undoubtedly true, as progress is made by the few convincing the many and because the experience of the few becomes the experience of society. But it is also true that the freedom of the many is often limited by "artificial" majorities on which a minority succeeds in imposing an opinion, or worse still, imposes on the majority who support them the illusion of an attainable advantage, while in reality this majority is being deprived of personal responsibility—and without responsibility, how can freedom exist?

82

To clarify Hayek's concept cited in the previous paragraph, it is enough to think of the anxiety of many governments to themselves satisfy the needs of their citizens. For the services that only the State can provide (public order, defense…) the only problems are efficacy and efficiency (cost vs. benefit). For other general services, where there is a problem of a service cost that cannot (wholly) be supported by all private citizens, the government tackles the problem of how to enable everyone to benefit from the service. I refer above all to education and health. The most sensible solution would seem to be leaving those services to private citizens, in a competitive system, with the State only taking the responsibility for monitoring them and paying the difference for those who cannot afford them. But instead,

State monopolies deprive the weakest strata of the population: those who have no alternative.

83

I must say that if there is one speech I disagree with, though it has gone down in history (because of its demagogy), it is that of J.F. Kennedy, the 34th President of the U.S.A., (1917-1963): "Ask not what your country can do for you; ask what you can do for your country." So we must not only defend ourselves from the government's interference in our lives and put up with its frequent inefficiencies, but also do something more for it? Perhaps yes: help it to "slim down" (see my book, written with A. Mingardi, on fair competition, ed. Università Bocconi 2007).

84

If we hope to reduce the power of the State (in Italy), I have the impression that reforms are not enough, nor are continual new elections in the hope that a non-existent two-party system will come about. I fear we have come to the point where this will only be possible if we cede power to Europe [the European Union]. Italy is like a badly-run company that does not want to change management and does not want to be sold or restructured. It can only be the subject of a hostile takeover, unfortunately.

85

Laws that determine the efficiency or inefficiency of its applications regulate the economy, but these laws are not automatically concerned in the long run with advantages for the weakest. It is the State which, in gathering resources (taxes), should be concerned with correcting economic imbalances to achieve a fair distribution of these resources in the name of justice and solidarity. The State, however, seems to want to sustain itself instead, creating competitive models which foreshadow its role and increase its (useless) power, creating social injustice as well as limiting the creation of wealth and well-being.

86

Normally, in economic terms, a realist is defined as a person with a good measure of practicality who is interested in practical things, such as earthly problems and results, so much so that realism is defined as being interested in material things rather than spiritual or moral ones, which leads to a confusion between realism and materialism. Realism is, instead, the pursuit and love of reality in its entirety and integrity. This includes the meaning of things and actions: realism in behavior, moral realism. The humility of realism consists in not being an idealist and in recognizing that we did not create reality, and we must seek above all to know it…. before controlling it.

87

The disorder we see governing the world is due, in our Catholic vision, to a lack of supernatural perspective, which if it were understood and shared would guide human actions towards a final end. Without this order it is impossible to re-establish economic order, but why should we be surprised? If we all had a supernatural perspective we would all be angels, already in Heaven, and how could we obtain merits with our personal behavior?

88

Some maintain that "… things were better before, even when we were worse off." My response is a firm "no." Everything man has done to get to this level of well-being is good, but what counts is the meaning one gives to the present moment. It is stupid to be anti-modernist in principle. The spirit of Catholicism is by definition ultra-modern: it is the spirit of growth, innovation, improvement, and progress; it revolutionizes technology, science and economics. St. Josemaría Escrivá taught us how to be men and women of our day and age (without being worldly) in order to be effective, and not to sigh after the past. But we have to do this by knowing how to restore the Creator's natural order, otherwise disorder between human actions and their end is created. We must be equipped to succeed and have both an interior and an exterior plan of life.

89

A great problem in economic and financial affairs is that many Christians play at being Christians, and are known as "Catholic financiers or industrialists," maintaining links with the Catholic hierarchy, without living as Catholics. They seek to excuse this behavior by citing the practicalities of doing business in this world. In practice, their ends justify their means. Perhaps in this way they will get better results than others and will certainly practice some virtues, for example prudence, but I wonder whether they truly live in the light of eternal life and consider the example they are giving. The gift of faith lived out in in a totally coherent life (no matter what job one does) is the unity of results: practical and contemplative, in line (with our capabilities and efforts) and giving good results.

90

In practical economics, whether in business or in finance, freedom of action does not mean that we have the power to do everything in the name of individual liberty; the human will does not have the right to do just anything. Morality establishes this right and its consequent responsibilities. If actions are directed toward good ends and are performed without infringing on anyone else's rights, they are morally good; if, moreover, they are done with supernatural motives, they can even be holy. Man has the freedom and power to perform morally bad actions, but he is then responsible for them and must bear the consequences. Moral law is not, however, regulated by a code collectively accepted and established by means of laws and sanctions. It comes from the needs of our human nature, created by God, the true legislator, but such needs are strictly personal.

91

When man acts according to the laws of the State, if he is lucky, he does not go to prison; when he acts according to virtue, he is certainly a humanly free man; when he acts according to divine law, inspired by the Holy Spirit and in unity of life, he is a saint.

92

Even in economic behavior, we have the choice between Christ and Barabbas. Barabbas represents "violent and armed conflict" in pursuit of temporal results and satisfaction, an armed fight instead of an interior fight. Barabbas stands for the Machiavellian end that justifies the means and the confusion between end and means; he was Marxism or the Islamic model of conquest. The Christian conquers the world very differently, imitating Christ, the only true Master. Concerning economic behavior, the secret lies in the Sermon on the Mount: carrying out economic laws (otherwise there is no result) but with an end in sight. Catholic "economic politics" does not favor exasperated individualism, collectivism less so, and anarchy even less: it aims for a society of people who seek the common good, even though they are in a free market system (therefore in a capitalist system). Catholic economic morals approve of the market but not of materialism, and approves of capitalism if it is guided by moral objectives, as it was originally. Even in economic behavior, beyond not being a Barabbas, one must also not be a Pontius Pilate. Pilate did not act according to liberty and responsibility, although he had the authority to do so, and his end justified his means. In today's economic world I know too many "Catholic businessmen and bankers" who behave like Pilate.

93

Perhaps this goes without saying, but the limit of economics and economic realism is and remains: what is man?

94

In political economics, the way of our Western civilization is to take all events, whatever they may be (crises, developments, births, aging populations, globalization…) and use them to make political decisions, perhaps even with a pretext of improving life itself, but I repeat that this is done without knowing what life is and what man is.

95

The ends must always justify the means in solutions to pressing economic problems; when one is detached from the essence of what a human being is, one forgets the ends, and the means are not checked.

96

It may seem strange, but even in economic decisions the first principle we must consider has to be our interior needs rather than our exterior needs. Instead, however, it is almost always the opposite.

97

The capacity to innovate, to invent, to create something big certainly comes from man's deep interest in doing so, which is not superficial but originates in the profound meaning he finds in his life.

98

In economic matters as well, it is not easy to explain and understand simple things, for example: what is well-being? What are poverty, detachment, satisfaction, need…? Will anyone try to respond? Yet these are "simple things" we speak of and hear about daily.

99

We will never solve economic problems if we do not increase our knowledge, since otherwise we will never be able to understand what man is, and what kind of economy can be constructed without knowing that?

100

Why is man only enthusiastic about himself in material matters? He rarely wants to take advantage of intellectual nourishment, let alone spiritual food. In economics too, mankind does not seem to be keen on man, but on a part of it. If man really reflected on his special dignity, would he limit himself to making his economic decisions solely by the light of reason?

101

Man's nature leads him to take an interest in his needs and aspirations, and to fight for them. The problem is to help him not confuse ends with means in his interests and his ensuing struggles. To help him it is necessary to educate him: as St. Josemaría Escrivá said, you have to catch him "by the head," like a fish… You have to know how to interest him in the advantages of an economy of the spirit as well as of the world.

102

Infinite efforts toward individual formation are necessary to save man from real poverty. To save him from the other (material) poverty, the effort required is infinitely less: it is enough to base that effort on his innate capacities and give him freedom of action in the market.

103

The more evident true economic justice and true economic equality become, the more evident becomes the political demagogy of states worried only about increasing their own power.

104

Moral considerations in economics are the real test of the goodness of the end and the economic instrument (means) against the background of man's true and responsible freedom of action in economics.

105

Duty is taught by example and is learned when it is exercised as the very reason for one's existence. It is better learned if advice and correction are accepted, given that the reasons for one's own existence are at stake.

106

Freedom, progress and risk, and not domination and exploitation, are part of true capitalism, whose Catholic origins were deformed by heresy. No philosophy, political doctrine or religion can disregard freedom and risk in carrying out economic actions for the good of man. Mixed capitalisms (private and public) survive only as the private form generates sufficient resources to sustain the public form. Imagine how much more beneficial private capitalism would be without the costs of sustaining public capitalism.

107

It is difficult to think that there exist political economic decisions destined only to satisfy material needs, with no regard as to how these decisions are made and what consequences they might have. One who thinks this way has a limited and "ignorant" vision of the importance of economics for man, as the problem is an existential as well as an economic one.

108

Just as economic thought must be clear and coherent with a moral vision, economic action must be appropriate to and coherent with the thought from which it arises. If moral vision does not inspire economic action, economic necessity will form or deform morals.

Thinking is not about having ideas, but about being able to seek and find the reasons to carry out ideas.

109

In economics, thinking is seeking the sense of doing; wanting is choosing what to do and striving to achieve the best result. If thought precedes will, it gives meaning to the result; if will precedes thought, it gives justification to that thought.

110

In practice, there should be no discontinuity between thought and will. If there is, either the thought is speculative or the will is weak. This is the premise of great failures (of men, naturally) rather than the success of projects that are ends in themselves. Understanding this is not so much a (speculative) problem of understanding concepts, but of how to carry them out in order to do good the best way possible.

111

Great thinkers of economic doctrine often vied with each other in proposing economic systems that took no account of human nature. In fact, few economic doctrines agree with each other (e.g. laissez-faire capitalism, protectionism, Marxism, Keynesianism or liberalism), concentrating more on models to try out instead of satisfying man's needs.

112

I will say it again: economics does not produce good results if man himself is ignored; it is unnatural, however, for man not to have economic requirements to satisfy his needs, and therefore instead of scorning or exalting economics, man should sanctify it. Is this possible? Ask the spirit of Opus Dei to explain this to you.

113

This is a two thousand-year-old part of Christian wisdom, but it is worth repeating: it is true that we can only live in this world for now, but at the same time, we can influence it; we must also remember that we will not be in this world for long, and that if we become worldly we lose our humanity and the prospect of eternal life.

114

The more the world gives us new exterior results, thanks to our talents, the more we should reinforce our interior capacities to use these results adequately, otherwise what we produce risks possessing us. This, too, is age-old Christian wisdom: if we do not dominate the body, the body dominates us. As we ourselves are poor human beings but creatures of God, and the potential creators of something, we risk not being able to control what we have created. It is important not to refuse the illumination available to us by using distorting sunglasses that make us forget that we have been created for much more than earthly things.

115

In economics, too, a choice must often be made between truth and error, and in economics the decision is often about what we think is our true home.

116

It is difficult to do what we must, but it is more difficult to want what does us good, because the most difficult thing is to understand what is good. If everything is so difficult, are we excused if we make a mistake? It depends on how hard we try to understand things...

117

Sometimes our humanity seems rich in goods and poor in values: it could almost be said that body and spirit compete against each other, and if we let the body win and thus disrespect the spirit which requires different satisfactions, the spirit gets revenge by depriving us of the joy we seek from our corporal pleasures. This is, in fact, an advantage that helps us to reflect.

118

Originally man was made to work, which can be seen, if nowhere else, in his physical structure, and woman was formed for the privilege of loving and generating life. Then man, envious of woman, convinced her to work and transformed himself into a caricature of woman… becoming effeminate, even to the point of seeking to generate by himself. This has perhaps not happened quite yet, but we are not far off, especially if we consider that scientists are using their resources to bring that about, instead of overcoming the physical pain that confounds the conscience, for example.

119

The mission of the philosopher is to make clarifications or cause confusion; that of the theologian is to make saints or demons; that of the economist is to produce satisfaction or make useless things seem indispensable.

120

The economy, destined to satisfy man with its goods, is founded on theories which interpret constantly-changing situations, often ignoring objective reality, and these theories can offer man dangerous choices. This is why, concerning theories, it would be good if these were based on morality, if only to check the meanings of these theories.

121

In economics, which I repeat is not a true science in which a cause produces an expected effect, choices are made according to a doctrine, whether it be monetarist, liberalist, statist, Marxist, Keynesian or Friedmanian; but in the end, it is always one individual who makes a decision according to his personal responsibilities. This is where moral formation can play a part: instruments are often neutral, but choices never are.

122

Man enters, goes through and exits this life with his spiritual and material needs. He is obliged to face economic problems as a means of survival (material needs) but also as a means to fulfill his plans (spiritual needs), that is, as a means to act according to his life choices on earth: these are, however, always and only a means.

123

When man confuses ends with means, he confuses himself, confuses others and confuses nature itself. In practice he causes suffering both to himself and to his neighbor. Thus, learning to distinguish between ends and means is a priority.

124

There is an often worrisome separation in man between thought and will. Man (very often) does not exercise his will according to what he thinks and believes, and often while he thinks he is doing good, he is in reality only doing what is useful. In this way, man risks being or becoming what he believes he wants, and not what he should think. In economic affairs this can have grave consequences because ends are confused with means, and another effect is the principle that the end can justify the means used. What one *should* wish is to want to do what he thinks.

125

Since man's identity is reflected in his will, which is the reason why something can or cannot be achieved, the will as well as the mind should be educated. Here we see the importance of a program of life, made up of study, work, reflection, action, mortification, sacrifice and prayer. There is an Italian saying: "Between saying [something] and doing [it] is the expanse of the sea," but one should say: "Between saying [something] and the sea, there are the means to think and do good."

126

It is unfortunately true that between an idea (a concept) and reality there can be an enormous difference, making the idea unrealizable or even dangerous for the good of man: it is enough to think of Marxist economic ideas and ideals.

127

We must consider that in economics or business the contingent is the only reality we are faced with. This reality is a continuous challenge to our capacities to choose and work well. We must always contend with the need to act. Acting well in contingent circumstances implies a habit of correct acting, which is difficult if one is not educated in this way. Correct behavior cannot be improvised or opportunistic: it implies a choice of conduct. Moral vision gives us this choice of conduct, and moral vision is nourished by continuous formation: the aforementioned plan of life.

128

In economic choices too, knowledge is essential, but this knowledge is itself a means for making decisions. Life is not for knowing, but for being. Knowing helps us do what we have to do for the sake of our well-being. Knowing implies having freedom of conscience, which is the essence of freedom: being free to seek the truth. Freedom, however, is not a vain concept, but a continuous choice, especially concerning economic behavior, which is probably the behavior most influenced by the economic behavior of others, and the least free. It is therefore necessary to have a greater knowledge of the truth.

129

It is obvious that whoever excludes religious moral influences (regardless of so-called secular morals) from economic acts does so because he excludes the spirit and recognizes only the body and matter: in this way, consciously or unconsciously, he excludes the search for the "foundation" of good and evil, of the just and unjust. In economics, this distinction cannot be ignored....

130

The meaning (of life, of choices...) comes before the satisfaction of the senses, just as the capacity to understand and to will is a prerequisite to a suitable choice. How can anyone think that this can be ignored in economics?

131

Individual economic conscience is destined to clash with the consciences (or lack thereof) of other individuals coming from cultures without conscience, and it happens that the "bad" conscience can drive out the good. It is evident that there is only one means to avoid this: by strengthening the good conscience.

132

Well-being is often an appearance, not what really exists. Our true needs are not what they appear to be; they are what they are, just like our freedom, so they should be identified and reinforced in a responsible way.

133

It is not true that human nature is unchanging. It suffices to see human behavior and its fruits when materialism triumphs, even though material goods in themselves are absolutely good and necessary, as they always have been, even in the terrestrial paradise. It is the relationship between man and goods that modifies human nature: to use another biblical comparison, think of Cain...

134

Can it be true that the best results (for man) in the applications of economic models have been generated experimentally, instead of upon reflection that took the moral order into account?

135

Man is always worth more than the ideas he comes up with for his well-being. In economics, I would say that a heightened attention to satisfying one's needs is necessary; therefore, since economics is only a means, it is indispensable to reaffirm the ends in order to create a true form of economics for man, especially in the global free market where today only continuously greater progress, not a return to an agricultural civilization or a stop to technological development, can resolve our problems (e.g. economic, environmental and so on).

136

Man often manages to create explanations for the things that concern him, which then become scientific theories, accepted though untested by the scientific-cultural community (which contradicts science itself); these then become dogmas explaining human behavior. Think of evolutionary theories that deny creation, psychoanalysis which invents the unconscious and denies the human conscience: these two theories are enough to explain why economics with its socio-political-economic theories then produces "producers" and "consumers," or in other words, men viewed as means rather than as ends.

137

If we do not clarify what freedom is, it is useless to discuss whether or not it exists, just as it is useless to discuss whether something corresponds to the truth if we do not establish what the truth is. How can one do good, considering the field of economics once again, if we do not respond to these questions? I would have responded to Pilate thus: "My dear Pontius, is there no such thing as truth?"

138

In economic behavior, the more objective one becomes, the more subjective he becomes. Let me explain: he can become better (subjectively) if he is conscious of his (objective) potential perfection, which comes from the divine spark within himself, but in order to do this he must fight a hard battle…

139

Is an act or behavior good because it is economic, or is it economic because it is good? One can object that an act or behavior is economic because it is economic: whether or not it is good depends on the use made of its "economicness."

140

If from Descartes' *cogito, ergo sum* I arrive at the *sum, ergo cogito* of Kierkegaard, the Danish existentialist philosopher (1813-1855), I not only reaffirm my nature and dignity as a creature, but I begin to relate to the world much more responsibly and even with greater freedom. This is also true in economic behavior, where the assumption of responsibility for one's own actions has a concrete effect on the common good.

141

The free market is an example of how a reality that functions successfully (even if it is a relative human success) is made up of free decisions, and this freedom is inherent in man, being a consequence of creation. This freedom is the foundation of everything and is founded on nothing less than the divine will. Not even God can change our free will.

What a responsibility we have, then, if we consider that our decisions are real only if they are free. We could easily conclude that true economics (which has a risk factor) is not economics if it is not free, and therefore free market economics is its only conscientious form, since freedom is essential to conscience, and conscience requires freedom because life has meaning on account of the freedom exercised: this is the meaning of economics. Freedom guides all of human activity; it is the principle on which our lives are based, and it is not only a means. It is this instinct towards freedom that give us a hint of our divine origins. In this sense, even work becomes a continuation of creation; therefore work is important and should be done well; work should have more meaning for us than simply economic results.

142

Economic laws must work in favor of man's freedom, not vice-versa, and if this freedom were mature and responsible, paradoxically, laws would no longer be necessary. The order of things in the earthly paradise could probably have been like this, because freedom materializes in the search for truth and, once found, in the application of its laws that naturally incorporate and refine so-called economic laws. It is always thus, as finding and knowing freedom leads one to live truth itself, and which economic law exceeds or can differ from the truth?

To understand the apparent contradiction, I ask you to reflect on two points: 1. By whom were economic laws established, and how (and how true are they as laws)? 2. What is the point, or what should the point be, of an economic law? Since freedom, as a vocation, as an instinctive or innate capacity in a person is the source of the responsibility from which all wise choices originate (among which are economic laws), this freedom must have an end; if it has an end, the means (economic laws) necessarily become appropriate in order to reach it (without forgetting that economics is not an exact science, but only an evolved technique).

143

The politician declares that everyone, even the most simple, can understand the most profound truths without religious interference, and provides the people with a costly, inefficient, confusing, extremely secular public school system... The priest declares that if the most knowledgeable man does not understand the simplest things, he will not inherit the kingdom of Heaven. However, if the priest cannot explain these "simple" things as he should and convince people of their importance, he unfortunately leads people to keep trusting politicians and happily accept public schools, leading to forgetfulness of the kingdom of Heaven...

144

Over the centuries, man has acquired a mechanistic mentality that requires him to know a cause in order to recognize an effect. That is all very well: the Christian religion is a rational religion founded on faith in reason, which is a way of thinking about God—who He is, why He created us and what He wants from us. This is also good since God is rational and conscious, and He has certainly given life a meaning and a scope man can understand. Unfortunately, however, man refuses to recognize the principal "cause" (the love of God) and so continues to understand nothing of the effect (creation). Thus faced with a logical system that presupposes laws (economics, for example), he cannot accept two simultaneous and different causes (the will of God and human needs). Not recognizing the principal "cause," he limits himself to accepting the contingent cause, based on his perception, experience and capacity, confusing, for example, human "need" with a material need that can be satisfied. In his opinion God should not be a competitor in the choice of "causes" and effects. Where is our reason?

145

The contemporary Catholic thinker Cornelio Fabro reminds us that if the metaphysics of the human being are not accepted in economics, it is impossible to perceive which morals should be applied in economic choices. Yet, defining man as a "rational animal," referring only to his rational intelligence, is an injustice.

146

Economics concerns matter and man's bodily needs, not his spiritual needs. But I wonder whether the man who neither knows nor recognizes spirit really knows his own body: perhaps he knows almost nothing about it, even though it belongs to him, yet he establishes rules for it as if he made it himself. I have always asked myself how man would have able to create himself (if in reality he were able to do so)...

147

Already in some places, they have been teaching that man is a thinking beast, and is thus dangerous to himself and his surrounding environment. There is no doubt about man's beastly qualities: it suffices to read Genesis, but I would ask you to reflect on the gift that most distinguishes him from all other creatures: his original, innate creativity. In his creativity, inherited from his Father, from his Creator, the human being shows his divine dignity. In this creativity there is hope that man can finally improve the world by inventing, with this very creativity, economic models less centered on the Western model of well-being, which I say without a doubt is unsustainable (above all, globally) and selfish (in regard to the poorer countries).

148

At heart the economist is like a doctor, since he too looks after corporal needs: true, he does not cure diseases or transplant organs, but he does establish a certain order. The economist also, perhaps less consciously than the doctor, tries to prevent infirmities and satisfy the needs of the human body, which lives a short but unrepeatable life. Let us remember that our "well-being" depends on how we conceive of the relationship between matter and spirit, between body and soul and between the interior and exterior life.

149

Why are we not surprised to be alive, to be able to see, to hear and to understand? Why is it taken for granted that all of this exists?

Certainly because we are no longer used to reflecting enough. If, however, even after adequate reflection we were to continue to consider all this as normal, we would have to acknowledge that we are imbeciles undeserving of the miracle of the life we have. Instead, if we accept this amazing situation and still remain unmoved (we did not ask for this…), we would still be imbeciles because we would not be deepening our understanding of the mystery of life and not enjoying it to the full. How can we think we are significant in this world as scientists, economists, politicians, financiers… and influence the world itself if we cannot tell whether or not we are surprised? What response do we have to this surprise? Do we remain unmoved, or do we try to explain this surprise by making more sensible plans?

150

If we recognize that there is a difference, especially in the results, between two different behaviors when faced with a problem or an action, we have taken an extraordinary step forward. Our actions produce results; the way we carry out those actions produces different results. Now all we must do is explain the reasons why we behave in one way or another. If we discover that we do so according to what we consider to be right or wrong, we will have taken another step forward, this time an enormous one. All that we would now have to do is understand what right and wrong are, why this is so and what behavior should follow. If we could do this, we would discover how civilizations are born and why they differ in the results they produce, in their recognized values, culture, science, economics, well-being… I know it is not politically correct to conclude that no civilization equals that which was founded on Catholicism… St. Josemaría Escrivá writes in *The Way*: "How beautiful our Catholic faith is! It calms all our anxieties, satisfies our intelligence and fills the heart with hope." What better synthesis of the roots of our civilization is there!

151

The cycle of human conscience is complex and differs from person to person, but in principle, apart from the very rich and the very poor, the most common cycle is the following: in the first phase of life a person wants to feel secure and be cuddled; then he wants to be the best in school, then the best-looking and most admired by girls or boys; next he needs professional affirmation, economic recognition, and then (if he has a vocation to marriage), he seeks the joys of parenthood by marrying and raising a family. Afterwards, once the "material needs" are satisfied, he feels a need for knowledge. If after all this he manages to survive, he feels the need of eternity, he seeks the good and tries to perform it—if he still has time. Although it is true that life is made up of natural "segments," there are things, actions, and aspirations that must not be delayed, because they allow you to do better and experience your current life "segment" better, such as the need for knowledge, the search for the good...

152

In economics we regulate (with appropriate laws) only 30%, the "tip of the iceberg" that we can see, while we ignore or indirectly regulate (often *very* indirectly) the submerged 70% of the economy which represents the common good that can be regulated with solidarity, paying attention to the human needs of the whole population of the earth. For many of us, this enormous part of the iceberg is an unexplored region: we know it exists, but we have decided to relegate its solution to the future progress of science or a future economic cycle; in the meantime we satisfy ourselves with our selfish theories of survival, which are unworthy of our intelligence.

153

We are used to appreciating others according to the success produced, honestly and fairly, with effort, sacrifice and perhaps a lot of luck that we sometimes undervalue, because this is part of our competitive culture and education. This culture can also make us form elitist judgments about those who do not have this kind of success, even to reproach them internally for not having sought this; we decide privately that they did not wish to or know how to use the "talents" they were given. From an existential point of view these people might be far "freer" than we, leading freer and truer lives. Of course I am not referring to those whose "poverty" becomes their profession, a profession in which they "exploit" their neighbor, government institutions and even the big-hearted Church for personal gain.

154

The analysis of men's personal success can generate a new theory of "compassion" referring to men of success who are blind and indifferent: those superiors who despise their inferiors, the intelligent who despise the stupid, the cultured who despise the ignorant, the rich who despise the poor, the powerful who despise the humble, the handsome who despise the ugly, the healthy who despise the sick, the happy who despise the unhappy, the young who despise the old, the good who despise the bad... These people should be as compassionate, or even more compassionate, towards those who are despised. As there is compassion and help towards the needy, which is a form of mercy, so should there be compassion and help for those around us who neither deserve it nor need it, but who thinks about this?

155

I love progress, since I am convinced that it is the fruit of our genius and commitment and of our work well-done, but there is an effect of this progress that should make us stop and think: the fact that it makes our bodily life too easy and the life of our spirit too difficult, thus confusing our perspective.

156

Responsibility in economic matters lies in correctly valuing our own duties. Doing our work well, spending money appropriately, etc... yes, but there is a responsibility that our individualism (though it is good) perceives less, a responsibility that only the individual conscience helps us perceive. In fact, individual conscience alerts man to additional duties, so he makes a great effort not to hear it.

157

Sometimes we hear that those who truly live according to the Christian spirit could change the world. The reasoning goes like this: the meaning of life is not shown by our intelligence but by our will, which permits us to use our intelligence. This will takes the object comprehended by the intellect and transforms it into something that becomes an object, not of intelligent choice, but of love. The factor of love is not normally considered in economic theories, yet it is also a resource and explanation for human behavior, as are will, desire and need. True, it is not measurable, but are the other aforementioned factors? One could say that it is only mathematics that allows us to establish what is quantifiable or what is real, but what is truly real is unquantifiable and unlimited. Can I suggest the same excuse as the scientist, who when he is unable to explain a theory leaves it to be explained by the future progress of his field? The day will come when man will finally know himself better and he will be able to formulate a "scientific" explanation of the effect of "love" on the behavior and laws that should regulate life (even economic life)…

158

The contemporary French writer Georges Duhamel (1884-1966) gives us such a beautiful evaluation of success that I shall quote it here in full: "Value your wealth according to the importance of what you give." Thus can the rich man become richer thanks to the poor, and in practice the poor man can enrich the so-called rich man by giving him the chance to sanctify his wealth, on the condition that he opens his heart wider than his wallet.

159

One of the greatest 20th-century thinkers, Jean Guitton, reminds us that we "only entirely possess what we have renounced." This is evident, because the opposite would mean that we would possess "what we cannot renounce." Nothing else.

160

Blaise Pascal (1623-1662) writes in his *Pensées*, "Knowledge of (physical) science will not console me for ignorance of morality in time of affliction, but knowledge of morality will always console me for ignorance of the exterior world." Like Pascal, I believe that man was born to think and work, but if he works without thinking or thinks only of how to spend his earnings, the imbalance between activity and thought will lead him to neurosis and lack of success, because while interest and sensitivity towards so-called practical things grow in man (which in reality are unimportant things), the interest in important things decreases exponentially. Even when one is interested in quality of life, one refers to material qualities. As this distortion is so evident, how can we put such faith in the so-called *ratio* of which the man of this day and age is so proud, seeing it as man's triumph over the *fides* produced by religious ignorance, but curiously, improperly exercised in matters of reason and science?

161

Concerning the anti-historical and irrational indifference towards the acceptance of Europe's Christian roots, Blaise Pascal offers an appropriate reflection (although it was probably in reference to another more important inheritance): "Which heir looks at his titles and says 'These are false' without examining them?" Well, about 400 years after his birth, his own fellow Frenchmen were the first to neglect this examination, perhaps "corrupted" by the Enlightenment spirit of the French Revolution, which idolized the goddess Reason.

162

The effort made in an oppressive and tiring job, done not so much for a noble end, out of duty or for an important responsibility, but only for futile ends and aesthetic satisfaction, gives us an idea of how a correct or worthy behavior can have banal motivations. If he is not taught the meaning of life and of his actions, man wastes the fruit of his efforts. The same man, who by nature should be destined to know the universe and truth, and do things worthy of his nature, bettering himself progressively, makes efforts for banal reasons that are an affront to his dignity. Although he is capable of (almost) anything, being potentially either an angel or a demon, man remains a little boy if he is not formed and educated. According to common criteria, this little boy is a realistic man…

163

The usurpation of the earth comes with a declaration: "This is mine." Even if of dubious legitimacy, this declaration gave rise to the principle of private property. From that moment, this "mine" (in some people's opinions this "mine" was unfairly usurped, but in whose opinion?) was cared for, brought to fruition and appreciated. Otherwise, there would be many commonly owned but useless deserts and forests today.

164

A provocation: man was not created to work, as I have often said. Man was created above all to think. If he did not think first, he would work without thinking (without seeing the meaning in it) or he would think while working (cursing work itself). The dignity of man is not in work but in thought (Pascal's "thinking reed"), therefore man should work to think, and to think ever better and better, and his work, too, would benefit.

165

The [realization of the] meaning of human work, not as fatigue and suffering to earn one's daily bread but a means subordinate to an end, developed in Benedictine monasteries 1500 years ago. There the monks laid the foundations for organization and for the development of technology, well-being and even capitalism. But above all, in the Rule of St. Benedict we find the greatness of sanctifying work, imitating Christ who worked and seeing in work itself a supernatural dignity; thus work becomes a truly sanctifying value, which does not stunt but rather exalts those who perform it.

166

Economic crises become crises of distrust in the powers that have caused them, because these powers lie about the origin of the crisis. Economic crises almost always have moral origins, a fact that nobody wants to admit and which they mask with deceptive justifications.

167

When we bring up morality in economics, we are accused of starting a "religious debate." No, a true debate on morality in economics is the most rational thing there can be. Every type of economic behavior originates in a moral vision, and each economic act produces effects of a moral character.

168

If the nature of man and the will of the Creator are ignored, one loses a rational outlook on economics. We end up considering man as an intelligent animal to be satisfied only materially. In reality, man needs three things: the material, of course, to be able to live, work and follow his vocation; the intellectual, to be able to reason and to know and understand the instruments he has available to him, without letting them slip out of his grasp; the spiritual, in order to find the meaning in life and its actions. If one of these three is missing, man becomes unbalanced.

169

If the natural laws implicit in creation are ignored, such as hindering life and impeding a balanced population growth, an economic imbalance is created, not just a moral one. This is what has more or less happened in the last thirty years: the Western world's birth rate has fallen, which has led to an increase in the gross national product (GNP) due solely to increased consumption, debt, and exported labor, transforming the West into an area of consumers and not producers. If the population does not grow, and GNP only grows thanks to individual consumers, what also increases are fixed costs due to the increasing average age of the population, which costs can only be absorbed by taxes and public expenditure…. Natural laws exist, and intellectual Neo-Malthusians cannot change them without harming man.

170

One of the most ridiculous, absurd and erroneous contradictions we have seen in the past few years is to hear governments describe as "economic renewal" their maneuvers that directly or indirectly raise taxes. Each tax increase weakens individual freedom, weakens the economic system and reinforces government control. On the other hand, savings reinforce individual freedom and independence, but savings are penalized by taxation and low interest rates in order to transfer their benefits to rebalancing the public debt, and sacrificed in favor of the need to increase consumption.

171

I want to speak further here about point 44 earlier in this book. The economist considers three dimensions that should be in equilibrium: the worker who produces income; the consumer who uses his income to support himself; and the saver who invests his money to make it grow. If the economic system in the global world does not observe the natural laws of economics (for example, by not producing children), the effects will soon be an imbalance and the birth of conflict among these three dimensions. Man works and draws an income from an occupation made unstable by purchases (of goods which compete with those he produces) and the investments he makes (in companies which compete with the company where he works). When this conflict exists, the economist is unemployed and poor.

172

An instrument is and must remain a pure means to serve an end. If it takes on moral autonomy, it becomes an end in itself, and man becomes subject to it.

173

An economic recession could have a "moral aspect" if man knew how to interpret it and draw lessons from it—for example, recognizing that it is not the economic systems or the instruments used that are the true origin of the crisis, but the way these have been adopted and used. He would see that it is not these which must be changed, but man himself. Unfortunately, what we are seeing today is the opposite: bad systems and tools are being invented that make the system worse; the power of the technocrats responsible for past errors is reinforced; the Church is denied the right to express opinions on morals; and men who could change the situation for the better avoid positions of authority. This all happens within the Church as well—something I can say from personal experience.

174

If the enlightened leader did not fear public opinion which would immediately attack him, and wanted to courageously take up the subject of the family's economic value in helping the economy grow, his success would go down in history. The economic value of families lies in the stimulus, commitment and consequent responsible actions they produce for their own support and growth. From the moment a couple thinks about having a family, a process of professional commitment, savings and investment is started, which leads to the creation of wealth, aside from the family's role as educator, private social security cushion, and private health care provider for its sick and elderly members. The family takes on its shoulders three whole areas of welfare, sparing the State and thus creating wealth. From an economic point of view, the family is an investor in human capital, saving and redistributing income internally. The family ought to receive the Nobel Prize for economics, or perhaps even be on the Stock Exchange...

175

Immigration is convenient when it is truly useful to the immigrant (for whatever reason) and to the country that receives him; otherwise it is "political."

176

A question: if the population level of a mature nation stays the same for a sufficiently long period of time, how can the GNP really increase? One answer: only if individual consumption increases. How does individual consumption increase if the economy does not grow, if not by sacrificing savings and putting consumers even deeper into debt?

177

If, however, the population does not grow but remains the same, its structure changes: the percentage of young people decreases and that of the elderly increases. This modifies the country's economic structure, and the fixed costs associated with old age (pensions and health care) increase. These are absorbed by new taxes, which in turn diminish consumption and investment. In practice, a country that promotes a declining birth rate becomes less competitive, and if this country has chosen to export production to countries with lower production costs, it becomes ever less competitive, as it becomes a consumer and no longer a producer, with diminishing savings and increasing debt. When debts can no longer be paid, the country becomes a nation of persons without work....

178

The economic crisis causes a crisis in trust, above all because its origins are denied and the blame given to the instruments instead of to those who have used them. How can a real prognosis be made if the diagnosis is wrong?

179

Discussing morals in economics is not a religious debate: it is a completely rational debate. The paradox that I wish to mention is this: "To be completely rational, faith is necessary." Creation contains principles of rationality, and not observing them means risking two errors: the first is ignoring the true nature of man and the satisfaction of his true needs; the second is ignoring the natural laws which are the consequences of creation, which regulate life itself. If the first error is made, man is nourished only materially, although he also needs two other forms of nourishment: intellectual and spiritual. Man is made up of body, intellect and spirit or soul, and this error proposes to nurture him by simply making him a consumer. Consumerism has been the rule of the last thirty years, and is the explanation for the current crisis. When the second error is made, that of ignoring natural laws, the birth rate is low, it being supposed that we are better off thereby because a growth in population is considered unsustainable. A low birth rate means little economic growth, less work, less wealth and fewer families created, so the perverse cycle continues.

180

There is a two-pronged solution to the economic crisis: first, man's dignity should once again be recognized; second, natural law should once again be recognized. In practice this would mean that man's three types of needs (material, intellectual and spiritual) would be fulfilled; true rationality would be found in faith, and man, instead of instruments, would be changed in order to resolve the crisis. A return to the recognition of natural law would mean that families and children would once more be valued, which would permit the three economic dimensions of man to be rebuilt and reconciled. We recognize instead that the opposite is happening, with man humiliating himself even more with unnatural moral laws, and the instruments are continually changed in a way that causes damage (consider the technocracy that has adopted the "fiscal compact").

181

If the economy, which is purely a means, becomes an end and assumes moral autonomy, it becomes a dangerous instrument for man, and this is what has happened. John Paul II foresaw this in *Sollicitudo Rei Socialis*, prophesying that the instruments would slip from man's grasp if he did not have the necessary maturity to use them instead of being used by them.

182

The truly sustainable solution for supporting poor countries is to invest in their human capital. In my opinion, other solutions are transitory, if not worse. They can even be dangerous if they encourage the removal of precious resources from the poor country.

183

Accelerated, unbalanced, opportunistic and selfish globalization has produced an unexpected result: bringing emerging countries into the economic cycle of material well-being. These nations, needing raw materials and having to be competitive, will bring even the poorest countries into the cycle. All of this did not happen because of charitable solidarity but because of selfishness. God can draw good from anything. To think that the neo-Malthusians of the 1970s prophesied the deaths of millions of Asians from starvation… due to excessive population and scarcity of resources.

184

In relation to this I recall a common stereotypical response from so-called wise men to the questions in which science cannot demonstrate certain things (the missing link, evolutionism, creation, etc.): "It is only a matter of time." It makes me think that scientists will eventually recognize faith in God as the only truly rational thought. Wait and see: belief in God, in creation and its laws is only a matter of time…

185

Depriving ourselves of children to become richer has produced only one result: we have become poorer, more ignorant and more confused.

186

If man forgets the meaning of life, he forgets the meaning of his actions and causes disasters. Who is responsible for teaching man the meaning of life and its consequent actions? Are they, by any chance, those who should have been teaching doctrine?

187

In order to restore the economy, before fixing the commercial deficits, occupational deficits, imbalances, etc., it is necessary to remedy the deficit of logic and reason in government actions, but this deficit is growing. Perhaps these governments need someone to explain to them that they should learn what ethics are and live by them in exemplary fashion, instead of just talking about them and pasting them up on the wall.

188

To illustrate the paradox of the current economic crisis, I will use an old prayer book of my grandmother's, which contains a drawing of an old man on his deathbed who is blowing with all his might towards a skeleton holding a scythe, obviously a representation of Death coming to take him away. The inscription below reads: "Infallible remedy against Death: when he appears, blow in his face so he doesn't take you away, but do not stop for any other reason, otherwise you will die." The paradox in economics today can be represented in a very similar way: for too long, it has been explained that the "infallible cure for the crisis and not becoming poor is to spend, consume, run up debts, avoid children (who cost money and do not earn), and never stop doing so, otherwise the recession will continue and get worse, and you will become poor..."

189

It is my conviction that people do not always learn from experience. This conviction is reinforced by these reflections on the solutions to the 2008 economic crisis. We have forgotten that to resolve the post-First World War crisis of 1929, Germany started up its war industries again, with the tragic consequences we all know. The USA, as well, made many mistakes trying to resolve the crisis. For example, although it had an enormous but unused production capacity (created on the misleading hypothesis of GNP growth, identical to the situation of the last twenty years), deflationary policies reduced purchasing power and consumption. The crisis would have been fixed quickly if jobs, consumption and production had all been encouraged. Today the problem is not very different. Imagine if excessive production capacity were used to provide poor countries with goods and to help them grow... Who would pay for this? Low-cost sovereign debt underwritten by poor countries over 50 to 100 years, as was done to support various highly indebted Italian municipalities...

190

Ah, if only we knew how to learn from past experience! Let us reflect again on the errors in Hoover's post-1929 American crisis recovery process. Having gotten the diagnosis wrong, the only thought was to control the deficit. In consequence, the production capacity fell by 50% and employment by 30%. To cut costs, even firemen, policemen and teachers were sacked (costs had to be cut!!). Interest rates were cut, or cancelled, and so savings fell by about 80% between 1929 and 1933. As a consequence, income fell by 50% and consumption by 40%. Note that "charitable philanthropy" fell by 40%. Does this teach us anything about the errors of the past?

191

Still on the theme of not being able to recognize past mistakes to avoid repeating them, I would like to recall the nostalgic old monetarists of Bretton Woods, who to resolve the crisis are thinking of re-establishing the gold standard and stabilizing exchange rates to create trust once again between nations. It is a nostalgic solution based on the premise that economic instability comes from a financial crisis in an inadequate monetary system, but this is not the case. The current crisis dates from the fall in birth rate between 1975 and 1980 and is related to the efforts made to sustain the growth of the GNP, which was bound to fall. In practice the crisis is due to erroneous and inadequate government policies, and also to the misuse of financial instruments and lack of controls. The crisis has its origins in moral (or rather, immoral) choices.

192

If only these politicians and economists would study and put into practice the recommendations found in papal encyclicals, for example, Leo XIII's *Rerum Novarum* from 1891. It was first interpreted and judged as anti-capitalist thanks to its considerations on economic power. The American government was simultaneously implementing the Sherman Act to regulate the monopolies that hindered the functioning of the market. John Paul II in *Sollicitudo Rei Socialis* urged investment in both technology and wisdom, so that the use of technology would be inspired, guided and managed by knowledgeable and wise men who did not run the risk of letting sophisticated forms of technology get away from them. In *Caritas in Veritate*, Benedict XVI explains that if (economic) instruments take on moral autonomy, they become ends and as such harm man. This happens when man refuses values of reference and accepts a nihilistic culture. Even Niccolò Machiavelli would have repudiated this nihilism. In *Discourses (III, I)* he writes that "it is a solemn principle that to reform a decadent society it is necessary to return it to its original principles..." Well said, Niccolò.

193

As hospital doctors have a right to conscientious objection in matters against their moral convictions (abortion, euthanasia...), an economist should also have a right to conscientious objection in applying economic methods against his own convictions, when these are imposed politically, financially or institutionally on the role he occupies (banker, economist, manager, etc.). It is evident that this is a paradox, since these professions, as we well know, operate empirically: they are not sciences, and these professionals are not scientists. I maintain that the right to conscientious objection should be invoked when one is asked to support an obviously illicit, immoral operation (political, economic or financial), even though an evaluation is often complex: for example, can we consider conscientious objection a refusal to float on the stock exchange a company that manufactures pharmaceuticals considered immoral? Could someone who does not wish to support biotechnological sectors that experiment on humans, or hospitals that perform immoral forms of research, have the same right, or someone who does not wish to justify or support a bubble in property or securities?

194

The new form of religion, which many think should gather consensus and create a new common set of morals, is the defense of the environment. The environment and climate have become subjects that go beyond ecological thought. Here the nihilistic way of thinking is waging a highly sophisticated and unimaginable war: first it convinced man that he was an intelligent animal who could do anything for his own well-being, without rules…. This has convinced man that human life, and as a consequence man's actions, have no (supernatural) meaning, leading him to commit two errors: avoiding births (and economic growth) and polluting, errors negating the value of individual dignity, reducing man to an evolved bacillus, the fruit of chaos. Now some have realized that mistakes have been made, but instead of recognizing the mistakes, they theorize about the danger man causes nature. Egocentrism is the new religion that wants to save nature instead of humans, a sort of un-creation. Who knows how much he who rebuked God for creating the world and man, and who refused to serve Him, must be enjoying all this?

195

In economic matters it is indispensable to work on ideas before behavior, to prevent behavior from influencing ideas: think of the foolish ideas of Malthusian economists who keep making mistaken forecasts that influence political behavior and cause bad choices. On several occasions Benedict XVI spoke of the need to resolve the crisis in education. The deficit in education leads to a deficit in ideas, then to a deficit in correct actions, and then to an economic deficit.

196

A mature (Western) country must adopt alternative criteria to become competitive again and resolve the current crisis, obviously according to its own competitive capacities. It can try to cut costs to compete with low-cost countries: this can be done thanks to technology, but this is labor-saving and does not create jobs. It can do so by cutting salaries, but this reduces purchasing power. It can do so by changing strategy and producing high-value goods, less sensitive to cost and price fluctuations, but it must have the knowledge to do this. It can decide to "sell itself" to someone more able, in the hope of receiving help: does this last hypothesis remind you of anything?

197

In *Lumen Fidei*, concluding the encyclical begun by Benedict XVI, Pope Francis urges that the Church play a role in resolving the economic crisis. He explains that the Church has the duty to guard tradition, teach people how to pray, impart the wisdom of the Magisterium, and guarantee the sacraments necessary to man, especially Baptism and the Eucharist: these things are indispensable if we want to understand the meaning of creation and the meaning of creatures' actions. This is also the priest's duty. This is economics for man, and the real "economists" for man are priests. It follows that not only are good economists and politicians necessary for resolving economic problems, but above all good priests who teach us the meaning of life and the need to seek holiness among worldly things. Without a doubt, the Curé d'Ars would know how to resolve the current economic crisis.

198

Voltaire had clear ideas about very few things, but concerning what I would call practical economics, he had some. His heart belonged to the atheist or agnostic Enlightenment philosophers, but his wallet was Catholic. He wanted his wife, doctor, lawyers and servants to be educated and practicing Catholics, to be sure he would not be cheated, betrayed, tricked or robbed. Voltaire apparently esteemed the Catholics he fought against. A curious choice… if he had converted he would have made the best investment of his life: eternal life.

199

The economic doctrine that has inspired the choices (especially in the USA) of the last thirty years is the so-called Keynesian doctrine. Keynes, like Garibaldi, must not be spoken of badly, which means I will have to make an effort. Keynes taught that demand and consumption had to be sustained at all costs during a period of economic crisis, penalizing the inclination to save and thus overlooking the origins of the crisis. Do you see why economics *cannot* be considered a science?

200

Still on the practical disasters caused by the Keynesian doctrine, especially his hostility towards saving, which he saw as a reserve to absorb public debt when it became unsustainable, I would like to reflect on the ultra-Keynesian doctrine of zero tax (on debt). This provokes a transfer of wealth from the virtuous who have saved, to those who have "virtuously" gotten into debt and cannot pay it off, as if he were deserving and the saver were a parasite. Keynes invented the hidden tax on unfortunate savers whose wealth was transferred to rich states, businessmen, bankers, those in debt or even the bankrupt.

201

This "zero tax" is even worse than it seems. It allows governments to manage the economy without correcting its inefficiencies or resolving the real causes of the crisis, and also facilitates distortion in competition.

202

Max Weber opportunistically distinguished the personal ethics of responsibility from the ethics of conviction. According to the German sociologist there is the ethics of those who have a determined responsibility in a function, and there is the ethics of those who are truly convinced. How is it possible to have responsibility and practice it if one is not convinced? Ethics of a function does not exist, nor dos ethics of an instrument; what does exist is man, who can give find the ethical meaning in functions and instruments.

203

It is man who must grow and evolve from an ethics of responsibility to an ethics in which he really believes in what he is doing, and to do this he must educate himself. This is why today we speak of the crisis in education, because today there is a greater need than ever to educate people to face complex problems in a confused world full of sophisticated scientific and technological tools (as John Paul II well foresaw in *Sollicitudo Rei Socialis*).

204

An apparently trivial point: if a man and a woman do not have children, it is unlikely that there will be anyone to take care of them in their old age. This is taught by nature itself… The State can try, but at very high cost and with less than satisfactory results.

205

My skepticism concerning the possibility of resolving the current economic crisis can be clarified simply: if a problem is not correctly diagnosed, the prescribed remedy can hardly be correct. If we ignore the fact that the crisis originated with an intentional lowering of the birth rate, an opinion ignored because it is judged moralistic, we will never understand what success is. We must have the courage to face the themes of birth rate and the aging population. I understand that it is not "politically correct" thanks to the ignorance we have seen in the last twenty years or more, but ignoring it is harmful because only the family can drive a balanced and sustainable recovery.

206

Today a two-salary family has less purchasing power than a one-salary family (of the same profession and age) of thirty years ago: why? Because this is the consequence of raising taxes (doubling them, in fact) on the GNP, precisely to offset the costs of the aging population due to the fall in birth rate.

207

It is painful to note that not long ago people formulated economic plans in order to enter politics, but then people started entering politics in order to formulate economic plans. Today one would say that we are inventing false economic plans without being political. Ironically, all of this coincides with our losing our sense of the meaning of life and our actions, and the fading sense of responsibility towards the common good on the part of the élite.

208

Albert Einstein said that to explain and face reality, it is necessary to simplify it without creating the illusion that it is simpler than it really is. Knowing how to simplify complex situations is one of a leader's qualities, while claiming that something complex is in fact simple is the stuff of dilettantes. Today we understand that in the West people want to explain the economic crisis in simple terms, suggesting quick and simple solutions, without considering whether these solutions are illusory or even liable to make things worse. Simplifying the reality of this crisis means explaining that we have gone against natural law in order to increase the GNP. But just imagine how people would react to this explanation in a relativistic culture! They would ask, What's natural law? What nature are we talking about? and so on.

209

Authentic solutions to the economic crisis must take into account its origins, scope and duration, as well as the means necessary to resolve it. One must have a wide enough horizon, like Noah who, when he lifted his eyes (to heaven), went beyond his own horizons and saved humanity, while other men laughed at him and scorned him while he built the Ark.

210

A dramatic error of these last thirty years has been the drop in savings: in the 1970s, a family would save 25% of their income, but now they save less than 5%. Savings are indispensable to create resources for investment and financing, and indispensable for economic growth. These savings, a resource as precious as oil, should be encouraged, protected, esteemed and put towards projects that strengthen the economy and create jobs, all of which will indirectly give value to saving. From a moral point of view, savings are a family's guarantee of autonomy and independence, but today savings are seen as a resource for resolving passing problems; they have been sacrificed to increase consumption, and to be put into risky investments. They have become an object of non-remuneration to bring down the cost of debt (a hidden tax, practically speaking); they have become the object of taxation or property taxes to justify government incapacity. When they have run out, which will happen soon, we will understand that there are no alternative sources of funding.

211

It is said that the current crisis is a crisis of trust: I will never tire of repeating this because it is too important. It is true, it is a crisis of trust, because having been lied to about its origins and how it has been managed, we have lost trust. It is useless lying to ourselves now, as man's nature and his needs cannot be ignored, nor can we ignore natural laws that explain what growth and progress are. Man must once again be given the three things he needs (intellectual, spiritual and material nourishment) and the three economic dimensions must be rebuilt and rebalanced (the worker, the consumer and the saver-investor).

212

The idea that an instrument (political, financial, etc.) can still be defined today as "ethical" irritates me. It would be like promising to sell a "good" service instead of an efficient one, but above all it would be like thinking that an instrument can be "good" in itself. Come on! Even a hospital, which should be for saving human life, can be used for the suppression of that same life. If a layman (one who does not profess Catholicism) should offer and carry out real ethical projects, people would be wary of him, like the Good Samaritan, a layman who gave charity to the wounded man without knowing the first thing about right or left.

213

Reading the encyclical *Lumen Fidei*, I found confirmation of my intuition that the economic history of the world is the same as the history of faith in God. When man has progressively forgotten the spirit, giving first place to matter and intellect, he has progressively created an ever more material and therefore egotistical and unstable form of well-being. The world's economic history is the history of the progressive widening of the space between morality and economics, and the ever-greater moral autonomy of economic tools. Believing that economics has moral autonomy has led man to believe that moral economics is an oxymoron; worse, he has been led to believe that the economy does better without religious faith (unless it is the Protestant faith, of course). As faith without truth is only illusion and sentiment, so economics without truth, which enlightens its use, is a betrayal of man; if instead, the economic instruments were sanctified, man could change the world, because he would be using economics to fulfill God's plans.

214

Economics, thanks to faith, can develop the structure of human relationships, keeping them united. It can create conditions for a true common good. It can reinforce that (even economic) nucleus of the family which creates riches when it produces children and educates them. It can create economic value for society when it respects creation, as it should. In practice, it restores an economy based on creation and its laws, on the dignity of man and the meaning of life.

215

Reading the "intelligent proposals" of slowing down the economy by a renewed fall in birth rate and the devaluation of the family, I recognize that there are no limits to the loss of wisdom suffered by our post-modern nihilistic society. If we "shrink" the population, first of all we must eliminate all the over-60s (whom we can no longer maintain), who are, however, a relative majority of the population. Those over 60 could hold a referendum on a law to forbid attacks on old age, making this a moral standard. Can you see that this "intelligent proposal" could even paradoxically produce truly appropriate and useful solutions?

216

What great power demagogic expressions have in a world where thoughts and ideas have been relativized! Think of the errors caused by confusing ends with means. Think of how many good ends people have tried to reach by bad means, for example by sustaining the poorer strata of the population with public assistance (which weakens the individual). Think of the power of falsehoods, for example, that a country's economic power has been restored (by raising taxes…), or that its GNP has increased (by transforming savings into consumption…).

217

Is the welfare state an end (for those who run it) or a means to support the weakest? If it is a means, it has failed as it has cost twice what it has given, destroying social systems by damaging the weakest, and has created unsustainable public debt. As an end, it has been "the end" of those who have run it badly. It is thus important to distinguish between ends and means...

218

Is the abuse of taxation an end or a means of redistributing income and paying for public services? If it is a means, it has failed, as it has damaged the system of production, purchasing power and consumption. Public services have broken down and are now paid for directly by citizens. As an end, however, it has been our end.

219

Is the policy of "involuntary" immigration an end or a means? If we consider it as a means to raise the birth rate in developed countries, to enlarge the workforce, or even for humanitarian reasons, we must realize that it has half-failed. The country is still full of window washers, beggars, salesmen and benefit-drawing unemployed people who cost more than they contribute. Will we see that this "involuntary" immigration has been anything but humanitarian and economical?

220

In economic history we have progressively tried to oust moral authority from making choices, presuming that this gives man greater freedom. In the history of the last two hundred years of our civilization, the opposite has happened: having turned our backs on it, we have felt the need of a true form of moral authority, but we have not found it. The world needs a credible moral authority that can clearly explain what good and evil are, and why.

221

The paradox of work in this post-modern, post-crisis age, has led us to make some truly interesting considerations. In the last thirty years, wishing to help the economy develop without having children, we have decided to consume more; in order to do this, we have transferred production to lower-cost countries, deindustrializing, and as a consequence creating generic and often unproductive jobs in the service sector. After the crisis we realized that we would have to re-industrialize in order to create jobs, but to do that we now realize we have to invest in technology so we can compete with the cheap workforces in the countries to which we outsourced our production. We have also discovered, however, that technology is *labor-saving*, and so does not require a workforce, so we decide to cut workers' salaries to stay competitive, but this reduces the purchasing power necessary to sustain the high fixed costs of the current market system, so now we don't know what to do… Ah, the power of economic science! The power of economists! It was better when accountants governed the economy, when debt had to equal credit, and the terms *strategy, synergy* and *economic value* were unheard-of.

222

Man has stopped using candles at night, but not because candles no longer exist; man has stopped using the horse and carriage, but not because animal rights supporters were against their use; man has stopped warming himself at the fireplace, but not because there is no more wood or because environmentalists put a stop to the cutting down of trees: man has always known how to progress by inventing something better, because he has a divine spark within that gives him the ability to create… but he has not been able to use this capacity towards himself. Thanks to Malthusian theories, instead of being more productive, he has decided to make himself extinct. Great. The devil should fear the *homo faber* [mankind as a maker] much more than the Archangel Michael.

223

I thought Cain killed Abel because the former was anti-market and Abel was too competitive in breeding sheep, but on reflection I think that Cain was an ecologist who could not put up with the environmental pollution caused by Abel's continual sacrifices of his herd to God...

224

I have thought many times, and I continue to think, that if priests had taught doctrine as they should have, they would have spoken only of God in their sermons (instead of sociology, philosophy, politics or even economics) with the result that our need to remember the supernatural meaning of our lives and actions would have been strengthened, and the current economic crisis would not have happened.

225

Question: if the population does not grow over a period of several decades, in a mature economic system, how can the GNP increase? Answer: by causing individual consumption to increase, first by sacrificing savings (substituted by derivatives), and then by putting individuals into debt. Why wonder? Man is not simply an intelligent animal to satisfy only materially...

226

Question: is greater wealth created by its concentration or distribution? If we do not have the answer, it is a symptom of immaturity of thought.

227

I remind you again that Voltaire said that the hardest and most intense work possible is the best way of preventing man from thinking. Man was created to work, but first of all to think, otherwise he would not be able to find meaning in his work: it is meaning that gives man and his work some value.

228

Work that has meaning refutes the logic of work "necessary" for consuming, purchasing, having and showing off. Work that has meaning does not transform man into a means of production, consumption and investment. The well-known "meritocracy" becomes a disguise to transform life into competition, to boost production and consumption. Man must be able to work to live fully and not just economically. Work should not take away the joy of living, and working hard should not force man to neglect other more important values.

229

True "meritocracy" consists of acquiring wisdom and merit; it is learning, knowing, thinking and acting while working, but simultaneously appreciating life. Thus man has value to himself and to society. Let us remember that there is a natural economy for man that must not be substituted by new false economic virtues; the contemplation of the world cannot be selfish and utilitarian.

230

We should reassess our idea of well-being and how it is measured. Merely material well-being promotes a life without meaning. Virtues are measurable, and we can see this by reflecting on the following: do economic development and wealth precede the ability to found families and have children, or does the courage to found families and have children create economic development?

231

The Church and her values are indispensable in economics, not only because she has inspired modern economic thought, thanks to her recent scholastic theologians, but also because without her works of spiritual and material charity, the world would not have made it this far. I am convinced that most criticisms of the Church concerning the economic resources that enable her to perform these works are due to those merits of hers that the temporal world does not want to admit or recognize in her. In the eyes of this world, the Church should just simply disappear.

232

To resolve the crisis it is vital to first resolve the emergency in education. We have allowed "how" to be taught for too long, when we should be learning the "whys: we should ask ourselves the reasons behind actions, results and consequences. At one time this model was one of our culture's competitive advantages. We must go back to teaching Aristotelian syllogisms: this would allow us to plan for the future, to foresee and correctly weigh economic choices.

233

Pope John Paul II was an expert, not only in general ethics but also in economic ethics. In two encyclicals he taught the basis for globalization, but this was unfortunately ignored (which, alas, happens with most encyclicals). In *Centesimus Annus* he explained what ethical capitalism is: recognizing the importance of the market, respecting other alternatives but emphasizing personal liberty in the economic sphere so that people can truly be themselves, fulfill their own potential and guarantee solidarity with their own peers. But he encouraged the pursuit of this freedom only if the individual were placed at the center of political choices. The ethical sense of capitalism means giving capitalism, which is a means, a meaning and an end. When the State performs economics it risks reducing personal freedom because in economics the State is both a player and a referee, making rules and competing, thus reframing individual responsibility and the capacity to take risks and make use of opportunities.

234

In his second encyclical, *Sollicitudo Rei Socialis*, John Paul II exhorts us to use the instruments of economics responsibly, or they will escape our control. To do this, man must grow in wisdom as much as in knowledge and skill.

235

The affirmation of the economic instrument's moral autonomy has had an irreparable impact on its ethical use. Is it ethical to tinker with population control to influence economic cycles and general equilibrium? Is it ethical to propose and impose consumerist development to increase the GNP? Is it ethical to absorb the social costs of an aging population by the growth of consumerism? Is it ethical to transform savers into consumers, into debtors and buyers of the superfluous? Is it ethical to double taxes on the GNP in thirty years to absorb the costs of an aging population and debt? Is it ethical to de-industrialize and de-localize just to import cheap goods while increasing job vulnerability? Is it ethical to force workers to go seeking work wherever it is created? Is it ethical to use savings to finance unsustainable development? Is it ethical to produce industrial and financial models subject to uncontrollable risks? No, none of this is ethical, but when the alarm was sounded the answers were always of the same relativistic type: what is ethics? We have the results in front of us: poverty and distrust.

236

The result of the answer to "what is ethics" has produced a negative revolution, forcing individuals to become state subsidiaries instead of the opposite. They have become subsidiaries to the state's need for false and opportunistic economic growth.

237

The moral meaning of economic responsibility shows us that it is not so much capitalism or the market that should be blamed, but the loss of morality. If it is true that economic behavior is regulated by thoughts and ideas, we should recognize that both are lacking or even that both have been corrupted. If there is a crisis of ideas, and this is transformed into actions, those who inspired these ideas should feel the sense of blame. It is nihilistic thought that has caused confusion, desacralizing man and reducing him to an intelligent animal to be satisfied only materially. St. Augustine wrote that from East to West there lay a sick giant infected by a universal virus that infects people's ideas and behavior rather than their bodies. This is nihilism, which undermines natural reference points in economics and its laws and is the enemy of economics for man.

238

Yes, there is a moral crisis at the base of this economic crisis, and there is a crisis based on the belief that only total freedom, even if it is irresponsible and ignorant, can lead us to the truth, instead of the opposite. Even Bertrand Russell wrote prophetically that without civic moral sense communities would disappear, and without individual moral sense, people's survival would be worthless.

239

In order for a mature economic system to grow sustainably, not just temporarily or opportunistically, and without "creativity" in the use of economic-financial tools (which create "bubbles"), we must recognize certain values which are not necessarily purely economic and which our culture lost a long time ago. The first is to recognize the meaning of human life; as a consequence, the second is to go back to believing and investing in the family and children; the third is investing in education and training, with preference given to "knowing-why" instead of "knowing-how"; the fourth is to once again value the entrepreneur, with his personal vocation to risk, and with his courage; the fifth is reuniting man's three economic dimensions, resolving the conflict between man as producer, consumer and investor.

240

The disparities in the following principles show how difficult the program suggested in Principle 240 are:

- Too many people consider man an intelligent but selfish and dangerous animal, the cancer of the universe, whose growth in numbers should be discouraged as he exploits and wastes natural resources, pollutes, etc.
- Too many people consider the family an artificial or even unnatural reality, invented by priests, where selfishness and diffidence towards an egalitarian society are taught, and where a partisan education is instilled instead of a global one.
- Too many even want an education founded on the "how" instead of the "why," hoping thus to form persons who work hard but think little.
- Too many people do not want the entrepreneur to exist, accusing him of being an obstacle to the growth of his own business, of his "economic value" being useful for the financial markets, because by nature the entrepreneur does not want his business transformed into a "financial product" to be maximized (milked), and he opposes treating his workers, whom he often considers almost as his own children, anonymously and homogeneously.
- Too many people consider economic growth politically, seeing it as the result of government success, thus supporting temporary, opportunistic, speculative and illusory economic growth periods, like that of the last thirty years, oriented towards deindustrialization, delocalization, and consumerism with its associated debts, which has made man weak and vulnerable.

These "too many people" are against rethinking these principles, especially since today a government no longer has the sovereignty to decide, nor the people to vote.

241

The penalization of the family and its relational and educational collapse have unlimited costs for society. Abandoning the family will be the definitive shift of our civilization and the certainty that all future economic plans will be inconsistent.

242

In order to compensate for demographic imbalance, it has been decided not to let workers retire, so the State does not have to take on the related costs, but if a worker is forced to work longer so as not to raise costs, this means no new jobs are created, therefore from one point of view, old people's lives are extended, but from another the possibilities to have others work in their place are reduced. It is necessary to "get rid of" these expensive old people...

243

Some would like the solution to the Western world's economic crisis to be resolved by imposing the Islamic principles of finance. Its supporters back it in many ways, the first being that Islamic economic ethics are very similar to Catholic, medieval and Thomistic ethics. It is true that this Islamic form (Sharia) does not discourage the creation of wealth, but only usury and avarice. It does not even discourage consumerism, forbidding only waste and useless luxuries. It does not discourage commerce or private property, but only stipulates that they must have an end. Should we all convert to Islam (as Guenon did and as other famous intellectuals are doing)? Let us read the next paragraph.

244

If we look at the state of economic progress in Islamic countries, it is hard to find exemplary results to inspire us and lead us to apply Islamic economic ethics to ourselves, partly because in countries where wealth has been generated by petroleum, we, not they, have invested in it. Is this perhaps because progress is "appreciated" more here? I will now try to interpret why Islamic ethics is not easily applicable to the global economy. One obstacle is because this ethics is imposed by law of the Qu'ran, not proposed to one's free conscience and individual liberty. In Islam we could say that even what is Caesar's is given to God. We know that some think this is true of the Catholic world as well, but at least free choice is given here. In

Islam, crime and sin are the same thing. For Islam, economic ethics seems to be imposed to avoid sin, implying a certain mistrust of man's capacity to exercise virtue in the material world. Islam seems to necessitate rigid laws that impose virtuous behavior, while we Catholics, identifying with Christ, must choose this behavior, but we succeed in doing so with difficulty... Would we, who are ever less Catholic and ever more nihilist, do well to follow these norms? We shall see in the following paragraph.

245a

We Catholics in this secularized age, in which people live as if God does not exist, where people go to Mass (if they go) as if it were a ritual instead of the Sacrifice of Christ, as if the Eucharist did not contain the Real Presence, are permeated with materialism. We feel free to sin in a pluralistic, relativistic and nihilistic society: perhaps this is why the Islamic world looks at us with a certain diffidence, or, I could say, even with scorn. Perhaps in their eyes we have lost sight of the ends, changing ends into means? Are they wrong?

245b

Which capitalistic model, developed with Christian roots in the Western world, has really failed? I believe that it originated in a model that was no longer Catholic but was modified by the heresy of the Reformation, which while considering human nature irredeemably corrupted by original sin, invited people to "do and work" in economics too, without hesitation, only to then correct (or trying to correct) things if they went wrong. In a global world where we are faced with many different ethics, this model has generated successes and conflicts in economic competition. Curiously, Islam also seems to consider human nature as corrupt but, differently from the Protestant vision, does not want to permit man to sin and thus invites man "not to do" anything unless it is established by the law. We will try to draw conclusions in the next paragraph.

246

Catholic ethics has a moral perspective in economics which is (alas, potentially) applicable with extraordinary results.... However, this greatness has been ignored and forgotten, doubtless because the Catholic has not known how to be exemplary in the use of the tools he has. Catholicism teaches that wealth is produced through the exercise of personal virtue: it was Christianity that originally transformed the formation of capital by violence (slavery, tyranny) into forming it through the practice of virtue (work, study, sacrifice, prayer). Catholic ethics has salvation as its end and teaches how to distinguish ends from means. Catholicism believes in the Incarnation and that man was created *ut operaretur*, able to obtain the virtues necessary to work well for himself and the common good. The Catholic believes that economics is a means that is good if used well—just like scientific knowledge. He is convinced that capitalism is inspired by Catholic principles, such as liberty and personal responsibility. He does not hold that these principles are difficult to apply because nature is corrupt and unable to do good, but rather that this nature is always struggling against sin. Catholic morality does not see materialism as a direct attack on its values, but as a deformation of the pursuit of progress, and sees the need for intellectual, and above all spiritual, reinforcement.

247

If the world were to lose Catholic morality and accept Catholic culture only on account of its usefulness, it would become an unsustainable social ethic. It would be like thinking that one is able to observe the Ten Commandments, but excluding the First: if this is ignored, the other nine are not easily sustainable.

248

Differently from Islamic ethics, which does not seem to have changed from its original form, Catholic ethics has suffered various wounds which have deformed its original teachings: it has endured the Protestant Reformation, the Enlightenment, Marxism, and even the Keynesian scientific solution of moral autonomy in economics. On the other hand, the Austrian school of economics is a successor of the sixteenth-century Catholic school of Salamanca, which "invented" modern economics after the discovery of America.

249

The real problem that makes it difficult to think of ways to reformulate Western necessary economic rules is that we no longer perform spiritual exercises. Thus we confuse truth and obfuscate decisions. I suggest the six-day spiritual exercises of St. Ignatius, carried out in silence, as a way to overcome the crisis.

250

Instead of igniting Keynes' "animal spirit," it would be better to ignite the "humanitarian spirit" of Benedict XVI. Instead of counting on the "invisible hand" of Adam Smith, it would be more opportune to count on the "visible and charitable hand" of Benedict.

251

For too many "intellectuals," Christian values, scientifically considered relative, obsolete and unsustainable, are no longer those that unite the West; according to these countries, they should unite around the pantheistic defense of the environment, an environment ruined by that "cancer of nature" that is man. According to many of these people, the unlimited growth of the global population has caused the present economic crisis, but in fact it is the opposite: the fall in the Western world's birth rate has been compensated by greater per capita consumption, and so we have created today's situation of population "de-growth," lack of development and regression.

252

It is a curious fact that environmentalists try to protect the climate and the environment without a thought or concern for its inhabitants. The environment is for man, who must protect it for his own good.

Those who actually do protect it are those who love the environment because it is God's creation, and they do so in a natural order, according to natural law, which is also part of God's creation.

253

Unemployment and debt already assail the Western world as a consequence of the crisis. The neo-Malthusians who claim to defend the environment from man's threats say that this is the fault of the high birth rate. Thirty years ago the world had four billion inhabitants, and today there are seven billion: yes, but where has this growth taken place? In the Western world there were two billion of us and there are still two billion of us. In the rest of the world, thirty years ago there were two billion people, and now there are five billion. Who knows why they have started to live better than we do… Whose fault is it? The neo-Malthusians, who predicted millions of famine-related deaths in Asia thanks to population growth, are now blaming the Church for having encouraged childbirth and causing the problem. Instead, these people should thank the Church because if there is respect towards creation, towards the child and his environment, it is thanks to encyclicals such as *Humanae Vitae* and *Populorum Progressio*. Malthus, on the other hand, hoped for natural disasters to re-shape the human population. I repeat, it is in loving and respecting man above all that the environment is respected, and one respects man by respecting creation, and of course the Creator.

254

Nihilistic thought and the errors it produces are costing humanity dearly. In its various evolutions over time, nihilist thought, which rejects all values and objective truths, has proposed several unsupportable theories, for example, the utilitarian doctrines which, by separating economic values from intrinsic values, led to the collapse of the economic structure, which in turn led to the invention of value based on a good's usefulness as established by the stock markets and banks. Blaise Pascal wrote: "It is true that there are natural laws, but corrupt reason has corrupted everything…" Perhaps it has also corrupted our capacity to evaluate the goodness of economic laws. I believe this happens through ignorance of these economic laws, but this ignorance is also a consequence of neo-Malthusian suggestions, of nihilist cynicism and the selfishness of ignorance.

255

Ignorance in economics has produced confusion in the use of its instruments, which are good in themselves but are badly explained and used. Let us consider the myth of productivity (considered necessary in the global competition with countries with low labor costs to which companies have shifted production), which aims to reduce high labor costs. The instrument is correct, but its application is incorrect, with unemployment and inadequate work training as a result.

256

The well-known "finance without rules" adopted in the last twenty years has been an attempt to compensate for the effects of the collapse of economic growth's fundamental factors, supported by unsustainable levels of debt. In order to avoid *deleveraging* (forced shrinkage of debt), other financial levers have been sought (bubbles). When these have not given satisfactory results either, the responsibility for the crisis has been laid at the doors of this "finance without rules." However, ladies and gentlemen, this "finance without rules" is a political, governmental choice: the US government had even foreseen corrective measures (the well-known agencies Freddie Mac and Fannie Mae created in order to aid the crisis due to *subprime* mortgages, created in turn in order to sustain GNP growth).

257

When things do not work, the technocrat blames the tools and proposes a change. Here we see all of man's pride. There have always been rules, but the fact is that they have always been ignored and relativized by those in charge. New rules, on their own or with other measures, cannot resolve problems. Rules are necessary and helpful when carrying out strategic choices, but do not give rise to helpful strategic choices. If we wish to give an example demonstrating that it is people who should change and not the instruments at hand, we need look no further than the sacred sacrifice made by Benedict XVI in abdicating, so that the Church could once more play a key role in sanctifying the world. This was consistent with what he had recommended in *Caritas in Veritate*: in order to renew the Church's structure, he himself changed her Supreme Head; he sacrificed himself, a self-immolation, in imitation of Christ. Benedict XVI, the Great.

258

What is realism in regard to families? It is above all recognizing what the family is. The family incarnates human and social truth because it is what conforms most to the needs of people, men and women, and conforms most to social and economic life. What bad things have been done which have confused the family, which in turn have confused man himself? I shall try to explain in the next five points. Realism towards the family merits it.

259

People are no longer having children, and as a consequence there is no support for the elderly. Victor Hugo wrote: "Respect for the elderly and love for children die together…" We can add: if children are not conceived, if children are not loved, not only are the elderly not respected, but they cannot even be supported, and thus resentment towards them will arise, which will in turn make them feel unworthy of living.

260

People are no longer having children, and as a consequence there are fewer marriages which generate children. Thanks to the falling birth rate, in the last thirty years taxes have doubled, cutting incomes in half. This has above all made it necessary for wives to work, making it harder for women to marry and have children.

261

People are no longer having children, and to make up for the fall in economic growth, individual consumption has been promoted. How can the GNP grow otherwise, if the population does not? Without children more goods must be consumed, so we have created a consumerist society whose only values are buying, possessing and showing off, from which necessarily springs the nihilistic vision of man as an "intelligent animal."

262

People are no longer having children, so in order to consume and sustain the growth of fixed costs due to an aging population, debt has increased, savings have been sacrificed, and taxes have risen, thus diminishing purchasing power and investments. As savings have crumbled, the banks' monetary base, on which they base credit, has been reduced, and so financial "derivatives" have been created. We have discovered new financial risks we never even knew before, and great bankers and managers have not known how to keep them under control.

263

People are no longer having children, but to maintain purchasing power in order to grow consumption, it has been necessary to reduce the prices of purchasable products. To do this, production has been relocated from high-cost to low-cost countries, leading to de-industrialization. This has meant transferring investments and labor to other countries. Then we wonder why, to find work, we are forced to move to wherever work is being created. The answer is simple: we have become consumer countries that no longer know how to produce competitively in order to support the drop in GNP caused by the falling birth rate. (I will keep going on about this every chance I get.)

264

I repeat (and maybe I will say it again): does the egg come before the chicken? Do you have to be rich in order to marry and have children, or do you become rich by getting married and having children?

265

People think that a 1% annual growth in the GNP means that in 80 years it will double. An 8% annual growth means that it will double in only eight years. If we reflect on these data, we understand how a dominant country such as the USA cannot allow itself a "happy decline" while maintaining its leadership position over Asian countries such as China. This is without even mentioning the defense costs incurred following 9/11... This explains that period's features of exaggerated growth and high debt with its subprime mortgages. In fact, during that period the percentage of families with debt in the USA rose from 68% of the GNP in 1998 to 96% in 2008. This means that of the official ten-year rise of 32%, 28% was due to families' debt. As we well know, this debt was not paid off, bringing down the banking system, which was rescued by the US government while the latter had to nationalize private debt. The ratio of debt to the GNP rose from 60% to about 110%: this national debt was in part absorbed by the Fed (which printed dollars) and in part by (mainly Asian) subscribers who substituted the sovereign debt of European countries (e.g. Greece and Italy, opportunely declassified by American ratings agencies) with US sovereign debt. In the end, all of an economic system's debt becomes national debt. This is the lesson, many times recalled but never heeded, so that today, Italy is still blamed for having an extremely high sovereign debt, while ignoring the fact that its has solvent families (or perhaps this is ignored in order to allow their savings to be seized in order to halve the public debt?).

266

Mathematical statistical analysis in economics can be dangerous! The growth or decline of pro capita GNP can be used as a political tool to justify or correct government policies. This is influential, being a relation between two numbers, the numerator and the denominator.

If the numerator (the growth in GNP) grows more than the denominator (population growth), pro capita GNP growth is positive; in the opposite situation, it is negative… If the population grows less than the GNP, the pro capita GNP grows and becomes a symptom of a government's success. If, in a given period, the population grows more than the national GNP, the pro capita GNP lessens and becomes a symptom of failure, which could compromise a government's fate. I shall now give an example from history….

267

I want to compare rich and poor countries according to GNP. In 1960 the pro capita GNP of rich countries was 26 times that of poor countries. In 1995, it was 57 times greater, as birth rates in those rich countries had fallen in the meantime (so there were fewer people and more pro-capita GNP). In 2000 the difference was only seven times greater, as national GNP growth in China and India altered the ratio in the other direction. Do not believe in statistical data, which are necessary in making decisions, if you do not know how to analyze them…

268

The latest UNPD (United Nations Population Division) report states that in 2004 there were 56 countries with a birth rate lower than substitution level (two children per couple), while many others were approaching this level. This will mean an imminent collapse in systems of economic growth and social, socio-economic and employment systems. Without evaluating the morality of all of this, today it is unthinkable to ignore the NON-growth of the population, or the consequences will be geo-political imbalances and impacts on the foundations of economic growth. (The power of natural laws!)

269

Why should the problem of immigration be analyzed? For us Italians, the problem has been around for little more than twenty years, since about the 1980s' fall in birth rate. Accelerated growth in immigration has meant a tenfold increase (over 20 years) in the number of immigrants present in Italy, from 500,000 in 1990 to 5,000,000 in 2010 (those legally declared: illegal immigrants are thought to number 1-2 million). Half of these five million are from the EU, and half from outside it. Now immigrants make up almost 10% of the Italian population. Italy has shown itself to be one of the world's most welcoming countries for immigrants, although this has happened very quickly and caused imbalances compared with situations in other European countries such as Germany and France.

270a

We must, however, evaluate the different types of immigration. There are types that are desirable and organized (for labor needs) and others that are inflicted, which are of two types: humanitarian or illegal/clandestine. Then there is the type carried out by growing nations exporting production activity and its associated workers (as in the case of China). There are other types which have political or economic reasons, which produce situations like that seen on Lampedusa, which the Pontiff calls shameful, but which are shameful for those behind the situations and not for those who try to welcome these people.

270b

The so-called inflicted migratory phenomenon confounds the humanitarian political policies of welcoming people and valuing their unique human dignity. The desirable migratory phenomenon is confused with the current crisis that pits actual or potential immigrants against indigenous populations. In a crisis period, the economic consequences reach further: the opportunity and feasibility of using immigration to compensate for the declining birth rate is questioned, as are the social costs; the ability to integrate immigrants adequately is questioned; the sustainability of being able and willing to offer immigrants unskilled jobs when members of the native population are living on unemployment, is questioned; paying immigrants low wages for unskilled work which allows them to have merely a basic, unjust and precarious standard of living is questioned. As things stand, if the crisis is not resolved, the problem will get worse. It is unthinkable to see immigration and unemployment grow together, yet there is no doubt that economic development programs in these immigrants' home countries are necessary, as these people are important resources for their own countries. If these immigrants' home countries, which thus far export only people, have unexploited resources, a growth cycle linked to the development of "emerging" countries such as China and Brazil, which invest in potentially emerging countries (in Africa, for example), will be created.

271

The accelerated global economic revolution which the West has caused by exporting work and increasing consumption is causing unforeseen changes and new laws of supply and demand, new laws of competition, new financial and investment laws, new laws of professional training and development, new laws of value growth, etc., but also new economic-political laws regarding private and public roles in economics. Industrial and economic laws based on research into synergy, competitive volume, etc. can be extended to nations that seek to create new competitive and political models. In one hundred years' time an "equalization" of consumption, work and investment models may occur. Of course, the distinctive element will be a moral one: the anthropological conception of man in the different cultures.

272

Today (February 22, 2014) the third technocratic government in Italy in the last two years is taking office. The question arises spontaneously: what are technocratic governments for, but to do in an emergency what political governments don't know how, or can't do? I am perplexed when I weigh what these technocratic governments have done in the last two years, but I would like to suggest what the next one should do. I suggest a Nobel-type anti-economics prize, to award to whoever does the economy the most damage. I can see many potential candidates, but I do not want to put a stop to others' ambitions…

273a

When a public company (which belongs to a large number of shareholders) has competitive advantages but does not get results due to poor management, it is subject to a takeover bid. The management can see this as hostile, but it can be seen as opportune and beneficial by the shareholders who want results. When a nation finds itself in this situation, the laws of democracy call for elections and a change of government. When elections cannot be held or conditions are not right, technocratic governments are formed: if even these are unable to solve problems, a revolution lies around the corner. If we compare a nation to a public company, there is the hypothesis of a political takeover bid: using our imaginations, if a better and stronger company launched a takeover bid for another country, perhaps the incompetent ruling classes would be hostile, but perhaps its citizens, overtaxed, jobless, insecure and without hope, would welcome it. Are we sure we have not understood that that is what is happening, indirectly and subtly, to our country?

273b

Scientists normally say that one day in the future, science, which constantly evolves and improves, will be able to explain what it cannot at the moment: creation or evolution, for example. I am convinced that one day the Faith, which does not need to evolve or improve (but improves the man of faith), will explain the scientific illusions of the "Big Bang" and how we evolved from bacteria. It will explain these things to scientists themselves, naturally.

273c

Many years ago I did not believe it, but now I do: in order to stay in a position of power you have to affiliate yourself with a lobby (let's call it that), even if you are not up to their standards. If you are up to their standards, and thus useful, belonging to it is not necessary for staying in that position of power, but you must never oppose that power. You must pretend not to know of its existence or ask for anything in return for the fact that it allows you to keep your position, and you must thank them: if you do not do that, you must have a very

powerful guardian angel... I have never done it, but I have prayed to
my guardian angel far too little.

274a

Eight hundred years ago, St. Francis understood that work makes
a person grow, but today it would be useful to pray to St. Francis to
ask him to help you keep your job and your insurance, especially for
young people. The process of industrial exportation from the
Western world over the last few decades, changing us from producers
into consumers, has greatly reduced productive and competitive
capacities, a fact which endangers work itself. Now, in order to re-
import work, we must learn how to compete with new economic
areas of the world, but there will be trouble if we do this according to
their rules.

274b

St. Francis made a life choice, as a vocation, of complete
detachment from the world. This is an exemplary vocation, but we
can also sanctify the world and others by remaining in it and living in
an exemplary way. There are other examples we can take: take St.
Francis de Sales, St. Josemaría Escrivá de Balaguer, but also Bl. Joseph
Toniolo, a politician, banker and teacher who was married and had
seven children: a saint for our times.

I believe that the example of St. Francis should be prudently
reflected on in order to get through these current hard times. In the
Western world the economic growth of recent decades has not been
founded on natural laws (such as birth rate and balanced population
growth) but on artificial, short-sighted laws (consumerism worsened
by debt). This growth has created fixed costs and technological
demands that require growth, not decline! Reviving the economy by
reducing consumption would mean not producing the wealth
necessary to pay off debt and sustain the fixed costs the economic
system has created, such as health, pensions, help for the poorest and
the Third World, etc. We must remember that the "Franciscan"
model of economics has no fixed costs to sustain, while the
consumerist model, which we all personally oppose and not all of us

live by, has elevated fixed costs which require a growing economy to absorb and pay off, otherwise how can we afford pensions, hospitals, living costs, etc.?

275

Furthermore, we should personally live by Franciscan teachings in this world which is so conditioned. A saint of these times used to teach that we could live holy lives in the world without becoming worldly, and that it is not the wealth we manage that corrupts us, but how we create and use it; he also added that having a little wealth was not as useful as having a lot, since if there is great wealth it can do a lot more good.

276

One wonders whether St. Francis' choices were in harmony with the Church's social doctrine. Of course, his choices were extreme within the ambit of this doctrine. In the second half of the nineteenth century the Church was forced to express herself following secular accusations that she was ignoring social justice. This doctrine first of all distinguishes between ends and means. Goods are means, and the end is eternal life; man is central to economic and social choices, as he is God's creation and not a product of evolution from bacteria or the fruit of chaos. In his vocation, St. Francis detached himself completely from the means, thinking only of the end: God.

277

It is important to remember what Luigi Einaudi wrote concerning the Church's social doctrine: he considered it the third way between capitalism and socialism, able to ensure personal liberty and even the necessary subsidiarity and solidarity. He also understood that to apply it well it was necessary to listen to and follow the Church's Magisterium. Therefore, the response is the same: yes, the Church's social doctrine can help our country at this present time, as long as we share its principles, that is, the distinction between ends and means and the centrality of man as God's creature, and here we return to anthropological problems.

278

St. Francis taught us much more than detachment from goods as a vocational choice in the search for perfection: he taught us the essence of absolute love of the Creator, and consequently of His creatures and all of creation. Francis was poor, but rich in God; he was an environmentalist in that the environment is part of God's creation.

279

He also taught us something that it is useful to recall today: obedience to and love for the Church and the Pope. In his General Audience of January 27, 2010, Benedict XVI spoke about St. Francis, recalling the famous mystical invitation from the San Damiano crucifix to "repair My Church which is in ruins." Benedict XVI reminded us that this "repair" should be done in communion with the Pope and with the Church herself. Charisms, St. Francis' charism of yesterday and those of others today and tomorrow, are gifts of the Holy Spirit given to renew the role of the Church. The great dream of St. Francis was "a humanity more conformed to God's will" with a vocation of detachment from the world or of detachment in the world, but with the same spirit. Today this spirit has to be lived under a "new world economic order" where it is hard to find real leaders who understand that leadership is a means for the common good.

280

Lumen Fidei, the last encyclical of Benedict XVI and the first of Pope Francis, can be considered the programmatic conclusion to *Caritas in Veritate*. The latter opens by considering that due to the dominant nihilistic culture, which deprives man of references to the truth, man has forgotten the meaning of life and its actions, and thus instruments take on moral autonomy, escaping his control. The encyclical concludes with the coherent consideration that when things do not function (and society enters a crisis), it is not the instruments that need to change, but man (who uses them).

281

Lumen Fidei explains how man can change. With faith and the truth (which is sought and then found), man can change himself and the world, sanctifying it in the process, because he once again discovers the meaning of life, understands good and evil and can distinguish between means and ends. He knows what his ends and the ends of society are, and learns how to use the means, recognizing that they are to be used for the end of the common good. This is the rational faith which substitutes the superstition of yesterday and of today (the latter being technology), and also brings consolation, certainty and true freedom in the search for truth, which reason without faith cannot do and faith without truth cannot give. To find this meaning in life, man needs truth (understanding creation and the presence of God in history). Truth is discovered with faith and love of God, and without truth, faith is only a sentimental illusion. This is why faith necessarily requires the search for truth; thus faith and love, illuminating the objective truth, change the world, showing man that he must seek to change it, to sanctify himself and his surroundings, and even carry out the scientific approach according to God's designs.

282

World history is the story of faith, as God the Creator reveals Himself to man and makes him promises, but also asks him to correspond by identifying himself in Him. Man, however, prefers idols, which demand nothing from him and make him feel he is the Creator, so God has to give a demonstration of love which can change the history of the world: He gives a new logic to faith, coming closer to man, making Himself man, sacrificing Himself in the hands of His creatures, rising again and thus completing the history of salvation, defining God's total, absolute trust in man. He brings Christians together in unity, in one body, the Church. The Church thus has various duties. First of all, she must guard theology in tradition, to be able to explain the faith and bring it to life in time and space, thanks to the sacraments, prayer and the Magisterium. The Church has the duty to make faith the necessary catalyst of the relationships between men, creating the right conditions for the common good. This begins with the family, which is the joining of two bodies into one, where children are conceived, formed and educated, which is a value for society. If the Church cannot succeed in fanning the flames of faith, life's foundation will be lacking, since the meaning of life and of various actions will be missing, with the results described in *Caritas in Veritate*. This is the duty of the Church, and whether she performs it or not can be seen from the results.

283

Man has an example and a helper: Mary, Mother of God, the greatest symbol of faith. She believed, and in believing allowed history to be changed by the Incarnation of Christ. I have always called this help "Mary's economy for man." Faith creates an incalculable "added value."

284

Paul VI in Humanae Vitae spoke of the essential, anthropological and logical value of human life. This encyclical almost caused a schism thanks to theological reactions of those like Hans Küng or Karl Rahner, who were closer to the demands of the world than to Catholic doctrine: thus the neo-Malthusians had ample space to impose their anti-childbirth mentality, which almost brought about the destruction of civilization. A few months ago the newspapers reported that the income of Italian families had gone back to the level of 27 years ago. No, in reality income has grown deceptively in the last 27 years, substituting consumerist growth for balanced population growth, due to the illusion that people become richer if they do not have children. Nature, however, has demonstrated the contrary, or worse: without children, the elderly—those who acclaimed the goodness of Malthusianism—cannot be supported. When ideas are lacking in an age of cultural emergency, false ideas appear true.

285

In "boycotting" the family, the whole of society has been impoverished. It has become a system without ends or identity, where individuals achieve their own aspirations and natural vocations in an almost savage way, without responsibilities, often unconsciously, without ideals or aspirations to start a family, have children and bring them up. Thus the economic value of the family, linked to the stimulus, commitment and pursuit of responsible ends, is being lost (or has it already been lost?). These ends presuppose, from an economic point of view, a particular commitment to produce, to save, to invest and consume, but this type of family also produces healthy competitive stimuli in bringing up children, which is an advantage for society. This family, to which the State actually "outsources" education and care of the young, the sick and the elderly, has a triple socio-economic role: that of an investor in human capital, that of a redistributor of wealth within itself, according to real needs, and that of a saver, which is to society's advantage. This family should be on the stock exchange for the wealth it produces... (See *Lumen Fidei* Chapter IV to understand further.)

286

Instead of hearing proposals about how to support families, we hear proposals for "de-growth" centered on decreasing population and shrinking families. The unrepentant eco-Malthusians still refuse to understand nature and its laws.

287

To understand some of the economic and financial problems the Church is facing today, it is useful to reflect on the problems of the post-conciliar Church and the pressures she is facing in the secular world, especially in the areas of sexual education, same-sex marriage and birth control (cfr. Paul VI's *Humanae Vitae*). Defending this encyclical exacts a high price. Benedict XVI not only defended it but even used it as his basis for *Caritas in Veritate*: the Encyclical on Globalization.

It is our opinion that the reasons for Benedict XVI's "resignation" also lie in the hostile climate he endured after *Caritas in Veritate*. It was evident that rebellion against the principles of *Humanae Vitae* could happen more easily if the Church could be attacked over sexual matters (pedophilia, homosexuality), but sexual matters are individual; however, in financial matters, transparency is a question of laws, procedures and governance. In not carrying these out correctly, it is no longer the individual who sins, but rather the Church that insists on sinning by not complying with international norms accepted by all. When she does this, putting forward unacceptable excuses (such as loss of sovereignty, privacy, secrecy, etc.), it makes things worse, because it is not true, it is not relevant, because it causes the Church herself problems. Allowing structural errors to be committed in temporal affairs (money and assets) is almost begging her "enemies" to return to the Roman question of whether or not it is fitting for the Church to have control of her own wealth. Showing that the Church does not encourage transparency or that she facilitates crime (money laundering) and showing that she should not be rich, since she uses her goods badly, can give rise to many potential reactions. The first and most important is distrust of the institution's morality and that of her guide; this leads to diffidence on the part of the faithful and a fall in donations, and then to fewer (fiscal) privileges from the law and consequently more checks on, and obstacles to, her activities.

Now, a moral authority's value in explaining to the world what is good and what is evil lies in its credibility, and once this is lost it can no longer teach what is good or evil, for example, concerning sexual matters, birth control, euthanasia, abortion, eugenics... If the Church, in an area with rules such as finance, does not accept the rules and allows illegal activities, doing so for "sinister economic interest" (and not even due to individual moral corruption), said Church will be seen as a structure selling a moral product in order to become rich and wield power. The (immoral) means proposed to reach (moral) ends cause the crumbling of trust given to the world's greatest moral authority in all areas, especially in that area where control is most desired: in the sexual sphere, birth rate, families, etc. (See the UN communication of January 2014.)

288

I have often wondered who the Pope's "enemies" are. It has taken me some time to find the answer, because I have always been around his friends more than his enemies, but then this latter group sought my company in order to expel me. Perhaps I finally have an answer: his enemies are those who seem to do good with their actions. I shall give only two examples. In financial matters, those who "for the good and autonomy of the Church" do not want norms of transparency imposed from without... In more ethical matters, they would be those who refer to non-negotiable values to explain that in the world one must act according to other values to reach a synthesis of coexistence and thus avoid wars of religion. Unfortunately, the popes themselves have had to recognize that within the Church there are those who want to re-Christianize the world while excluding Christ, and therefore relativistic theologies triumph and a pantheistic theology creeps in, a religion of the modern world which "seems" to deny free will and the person.

289

Thus it is considered ethical to fight against the death penalty, world hunger, youth unemployment, discrimination and vivisection, while abortion, euthanasia and eugenics etc. are no longer discussed. When matters in the sexual sphere crop up, there is an unusual diplomatic capacity for not saying what needs to be said.

290

We do not always understand whether some people in the Church want her to survive or want to sanctify her; we do not understand whether Rosmini's five wounds of the Church have become six or seven, thanks to the attention paid to remodeling the Magisterium to better fit the pressures of the modern world (H. Küng, K. Rahner). Declaring that this world persecutes the Church and thus this Church must defend the secrecy of her accounts is something I would not believe had I not seen it for myself.

291

There are some who maintain that nobody could have foreseen the risks in global finance and the consequences we are going through. This is not true. Rather, it is true that since these risks were forecast by explaining them from a moral viewpoint, these explanations were cast aside with indifference. The financial world wished to give itself moral autonomy, and the consequences are evident.

292

Thirty years ago the impossibility of ensuring sustainable economic growth with zero population growth was foreseen, and people asked whether it was ethical and logical to apply Keynesian methods to managing the population to balance things out. It was asked whether it was ethical and logical to propose the illusion of "selfish" development based only on individual consumer growth. It was asked whether it was ethical and logical to think of letting the rise in consumption absorb the rise in social costs (pensions and healthcare), inevitably leading to tax increases. It was asked whether it was ethical and logical to change a people of savers into a people of debt-ridden consumers anxious to be able to buy everything, useful or not. It was asked whether it was ethical and logical to impose the idea worldwide that working close to home was a thing of the past and that it was necessary to go wherever work was being created (that is, where money was being invested).

It was accepted as very ethical (but not logical) to allow everyone the possibility of buying a house, even those who could not afford a mortgage and the interest, and so *subprime* mortgages were invented, with the consequences of which we are all well aware. This model became a Machiavellian example of a good end (a home for everybody) being pursued by bad means (an unsustainable and dangerous financial structure). It was then asked whether it was ethical to finance this model with the savings of citizens, which were often invested in incomprehensible financial products. It was further asked whether it was ethical and logical to accept competitive models centered on share growth, forcing banks to take excessive risks and be less than transparent in order to demonstrate growth and high gains.

In reality there were many questions, but the answers were always: what do ethics have to do with it? Which ethics? The fact is that these were all ethical as well as logical questions.

293

But what will be the cost of this ethical deficit? The first consequence after the illusion of wealth, wasted savings and greater debt, is that for a few years (until the deficit produced is absorbed), the banks will finance the economic system less, which will invest less, produce less, take on less and pay less. We will consume less, save less and invest less. In practice we will live less well-off, and we will be forced to accept a form of statism with surprises in the shape of whatever means are chosen to control the economy: greater taxes, more inflation or deflation, fewer taxes with no interest on savings, wealth taxes, pension and social security cuts…

294

Therefore the recommendation of Benedict XVI to detach ourselves from the problem of money is challenging and opportune. Our Pontiff reminds us above all that money is only an instrument and we should remember its ends. It is true that if wealth is not created it cannot be distributed; but if it is created badly, as has just happened, two values are destroyed: the value of wealth itself, and the value of man.

295

The fact is that capitalism is a sign of contradiction; it has advantages, but it can take on selfish principles that are exaggeratedly competitive, and at times allows for cheating. Sometimes it seems to impose choices on man (and on the planet) regardless of whether or not they are intrinsically good, let alone necessary, or else the system will fail. The inconsistent model of development over the last few years is an example. This century's economic utopia has meant that "more is better," causing degeneration in human relations.

296

To demonstrate this, the following question suffices: what value does the human person have today? The nihilistic response is: however much he can earn, spend and consume during his lifetime. Today almost nobody believes this, and a lack of confidence reigns. You see, in society the fundamental economic value of confidence has been forgotten, and it is remembered only when it is lacking. Confidence is founded on the ethical conduct of workers, and this results in a series of key behaviors. First of all, models of competition improve, which often are forced to lower themselves to the level of the most opportunistic and disloyal competitor; this then creates credibility, which in turn creates a certain image that guarantees the loyalty of employees, suppliers and clients. This loyalty leads to the lowering of costs due to fewer risks, checks and errors. It creates motivation and cooperation between collaborators, and with the lack of stress, productivity increases. It also gives the company financial value in the eyes of its investors, guaranteeing stability. In addition, it leads to human development; it stimulates creativity, true efficiency and results.

Today's market demands, above all, certainty and respect for rules. Disloyalty in economics and finance, which leads to the need for hiding growth phenomena, results and information from the market, produces an unacceptable collective cost. We are optimistic about being able to heal the economy and overcome the crisis, but if we do not manage to heal the lack of ethics by recreating trust, this healing will be merely temporary.

297a

Pope Benedict spoke about a "wealth gap." Let us first of all see what this means. It should mean that before the crisis, the gap between rich and poor was narrower than it was afterwards, and that this wider gap is its consequence. The interpretation is correct regarding this gap in the so-called Western countries (which were formerly wealthy), while it is the opposite when comparing the West with the newly rich countries of the East: the formerly rich countries with the formerly poor countries. Thanks to accelerated globalization, which became necessary to maintain the imbalances of the West (USA and Europe), the countries that used to be called developing countries have become richer, reducing the gap, while within the "mature" countries this gap between the social classes has grown, thanks to rising unemployment and decreased income, pensions, purchasing power and investment returns because of the steady, indiscriminate growth in taxes, etc.

If we look carefully, another cause is waning solidarity and almsgiving. We have said many times before that the fall in birth rate would mean less wealth, and this is indeed the case. Countries which have selfishly sacrificed having children for the illusion of being better off must now rethink this well-being, and quickly. The opposite has happened in other countries: with the unbalanced exportation of manufacturing, especially in the last two decades, our Western world has sacrificed production and profit (which is the opposite of what was hoped for in exporting work to boost competition), and it has invented financial profit, more conceptual than real, founded on the assumption that consumer growth is sustainable and the debts incurred repayable. It has not turned out like this, and the great illusion is over. Finance has been favored over labor because labor has been "exported" to where it costs less, in order to increase purchasing power and consumption. This was done because the real economy was not growing, and that was because there were no children. This is why finance, which has managed the key element of (bogus) growth, i.e. debt, has taken the place of production and work, because these were exported and because people were no longer saving.

297b

How to solve this problem is not (only) the duty of economists but also of educators. This is because, after thirty years of mistaken values, new, true values have to be taught. This cannot be done in a heartbeat with reforms or new laws. Changing cultural values takes time, and also requires capable teachers. Are there any such? Are there families who put their children's education above all else, who see education as an investment instead of an expense just like gym, tennis or skiing fees? Are there priests who above all teach doctrine and morals? Priests who teach people how to confess? Don't you think that confession is a true education? This alone is the first education, which teaches the meaning of life and its actions: the rest will follow.

298

Our Pontiff emeritus once again shows that he is a true economist, the economist par excellence, an economist for man, who knows God well, who understands in a unique way man's true needs and how to satisfy them through economic instruments. Benedict XVI simply reminds us of what he wrote in *Caritas in Veritate*: economics and finance are only means. These means require an end in order to be used well, or they will become sterile, as has happened. Our beloved Pope Benedict XVI explains this with the unique wisdom and ability that only he possesses.

299

In reflecting on this economic crisis' causes, consequences and solutions, I maintain that it is not capitalism that should take the blame, but the loss of moral sense. This is because the real origin of the crisis is a moral one. How an economist behaves and works in a capitalist system is regulated by his thoughts. If the crisis is in his thoughts, this will come through in his actions; therefore I maintain that if anyone should feel guilty, it should be those who had the moral responsibility to inspire this behavior. It is not so difficult to get to the roots of this responsibility: it comes from the nihilistic thinking which has confused the last few generations, with man being stripped of his sacredness and being reduced to the status of an intelligent animal to be satisfied only materially. I find it unjust to lay the blame on an instrument, like capitalism, instead of on those who have misused it through their ignorance. The business world is not in contradiction with the world of morals, and ethical and non-ethical thought; they are two different things. The first world explains what to do, and the second explains why.

St. Augustine wrote that from the east to the west there is a great contagion, infecting people not physically but in their minds and thus in their actions. If the spirit is sick, behavior also becomes sick, and here we mean economic behavior. This virus, this nihilistic way of thinking which rejects every value and objective truth and considers man merely as an intelligent animal to be satisfied materially, impedes man from performing true economics, even to the point of making him ignore natural economic laws and reject life, camouflage economic laws and cheat in applying them. In practice he subverts the laws of economics themselves, as has happened in recent years. Nihilism is the enemy of economics from man's point of view.

300

Now, as well as planning a solution to the crisis, it would be good to work on ideas as well, by relearning to distinguish between means and ends, by no longer attributing moral autonomy to economics, and by making those involved in it recognize their personal responsibilities. This sense, as it has been weakened, needs to be taught again, as economic choices produce important social and moral effects. It is "how and why" these economic laws are applied that explains whether or not true economics is being applied. This needs to be taught again, because while economic instruments have become rather sophisticated (for example, the well-known financial derivatives), man seems to have gone backward to less mature ideas of conscience and wisdom, and so these instruments tend to escape his grasp (as John Paul II predicted in *Sollicitudo*).

In causing and mishandling this crisis, the immature man has shown the ability to waste many resources instead of using them well; he has sustained incomplete, bogus and at times even just plain false economic development; he has not worked for the distribution of wealth as he should have. The presumed (nihilistic) moral autonomy of the economy has made us relativistically forget values and ethical rules, urging selfishness to the fore in the pursuit of pleasure and power; it has also made us think that ethics lies only in what is tangible, be that profit in itself (regardless of how it is created) or goods available in a consumerist, materialistic system. There is indeed a moral crisis at the root of this economic crisis; there is a crisis founded on the certainty that only total freedom (even if it is irresponsible and ignorant) can lead to the conquest of truth, instead of the other way around, which is that true freedom comes only from accepting an original truth. Without this truth, for example, we could attempt to quickly solve this crisis in our country with a house price boom paired with massive inflation (with obvious pros and cons), instead of with a necessary period of well-managed austerity, given the preceding unsustainable levels of economic well-being.

301

If it is true that the family was "invented" by Christianity, this would suffice to give the latter merit for the economic values it has created over the centuries, and we could award it a cumulative Nobel Prize for economics. Let us try to imagine the terrible effects on society if the family had never existed: it would be a society without ends or identity, in which individuals could not find their vocations except through savagery. It would then be a society confused about the ends of its actions, a society without meaningful responsibilities, aspirations, motivations or conscious growth. Maybe it would generate more children, but that would not be a value in itself, as children should not just be created but also raised and educated individually, and who would do this—the collective? If there were no family, there would be disorganization and social impoverishment. But is this why they knowingly continue to suppress the family and not support it? To destroy civilization?

302a

The economic value of the family comes from the stimulus, commitment and follow-through of those in charge, directed to the support and growth of the family: that is, the producing, saving, investing, creating of wealth, and consuming. It also creates healthy competitive stimuli in the education and sustenance of children and creates greater value and sustainability for society, causing the production of wealth in society. How much value does an educated person have for society, a person whose education is perhaps based on our 2000-year-old culture? Do we wonder how much was invested to create this value? Not only this, but the family tends to absorb all the social and economic problems of its members, preventing them from becoming problems for society (for example, its children's unemployment and the so-called "unemployment" of housewives). Do we wonder how much this help is worth?

Not only this, but the family tends to help, as far as it can, its sick and elderly, whose support would end up weighing on society. How much is this help worth? What value does the role of the family have for society? It bears at least three areas of welfare on its shoulders, areas that create growth and wealth and lessen the costs to the state, three areas that are "outsourced" to families and should be compensated by a type of "devolution" or at least considered "non-profit" and thus tax-exempt. Furthermore, the family, from the purely economic point of view, has three roles: it is an investor, as it invests in human capital and development, and therefore in the entire socio-economic system. It is a saver, because the formation of this human capital takes place primarily within its circle, which represents savings to society itself. It is a redistributor of income among its members according to their needs, which only the family has the right to understand and establish.

302b

Not everyone agrees with the above. According to many people and for many different reasons, the family operates to the "detriment" of society. It produces children (who pollute), whom they raise and educate (in a subjective, selfish way). It keeps the sick and the elderly alive (with high pension and health costs). It oppresses women, banishing them to the kitchen (and refuses to emancipate them)…

303

The family has an auto-productive role, due to the activities performed within it, and a super-productive role for what it does on the outside. This attitude leads to a virtuous and misunderstood cycle, which is the real producer of wealth for society. This role should be rewarded for its results, for example with bonuses for children and their performance (level of education, how much work is done, earnings and taxes paid…), but instead the family is ignored, if not actually derided and devalued, for the reasons given in the previous paragraph.

304

What is seriously worrisome is the fact that the negative effects of this indifference are ignored, while what I stated two paragraphs ago is considered true. Let us think of the decline in birthrate, which began around 1974, in light of the crisis of the family on one hand (the number of marriages fell by nearly half between 1972 and 2003, while divorces quadrupled), and on the other hand in light of the neo-Malthusian myth of population control. In two years this mentality caused birthrates to fall from 7% to 1.5% in rich countries, while those in poor countries, who do not know how to read such convincing books, continued to have children. The result is that nowadays we have to "import" citizens from other countries thanks to the impact of the falling birth rate and the consequent decline in wealth produced, due to fewer savings, less available financial wealth, fewer taxes paid, a greater deficit, and higher public expenditure.

305

The countries that, concerned about this phenomenon, set up family funds in the first decade of this century, managed to raise the birth rate with funds set aside to support this: for example, the birth rate in France rose by 2.5%, and the government set aside 2% of its GNP; Germany set aside 3.2%; Scandinavian countries 4%; Italy roughly 1%. Does Italy even believe in the family? That is the wrong question; to be consistent with what I wrote above, I should have asked whether Italy believes that an increase in families will lead to GNP growth, increased wealth, etc.? Does Italy believe that the family not only increases GNP but also creates benefits that are not just economic? Does Italy believe that values for society are created when the family is supported? If it were possible, as I have already said, I would float the family on the stock exchange, as it creates the most sustainable economic values there are.

306

No true scientist would ever have behaved towards Pope Benedict like the learned men of La Sapienza University, refusing to welcome him. Instead they behaved just like what they wish to be seen as (learned men), but to *be* so, they would have to accept too many "dogmas." Since they have to be dogmatic if they want to keep their jobs, they see the Pontiff as a fearful competitor in their fields. A true scientist is used to believing in experimental and provisional science, and is convinced that a theory only becomes a theory when it is proven and confirmed, and that a theory only becomes a scientific law when it is universally accepted.

No real scientist would fear a confrontation with or silence the Catholic Pontiff, who represents the most rational and scientific of all religions, the root of Western culture and civilization, the origin of European universities, refusing to welcome him due to his "anti-scientific" outlook. The problem with these unwise men is that since they are not accustomed to using scientific logic, but rather the logic that comes from the "Enlightenment tradition," they are more dogmatic than religious fundamentalists, more superstitious than members of a cult, and they see the head of Catholicism as too strong an opponent. They did not want him, and they succeeded in keeping him away, through fear for their well-guarded and secretive non-science.

307

There is unemployment among the youth—which worries even Pope Francis—because children are not being born. No children means no real and sustainable economic growth, a basis for creating true jobs. No children has meant a growth only in consumption. (If the population does not grow, how can the GNP? Only through individual consumption, which is consumerism.) Consumption means a reduction in savings (which has reduced the monetary base for bank credit), and families getting into more debt. All of this is accompanied more and more often by exporting production to cheaper countries, in order to import low-cost goods and thus increase purchasing power, but these goods are produced elsewhere. No children also means an aging population and rising fixed costs (health, pensions) sustained by higher taxes and less investment. The vicious circle created by a decline in the birth rate has been: declining development, increasing fixed costs, increasing taxes, exported production, a decline in investments, growing debt, etc. In practice, we have created the conditions for diminished competitive capacity in order to create jobs.

308

The only way to resolve the unemployment problem is to create true economic development, but it does not seem easy. There are no serious projects in the offing. In addition, the state does not have the resources (and cannot create them due to financial constraints), the private sector does not want to take risks, and foreign capital investors are not interested. More numerous jobs, which would mean our being competitive again, would be difficult because for the West to compete with the East, the only solution would seem to lie in technology, and technology does not require a large workforce, as we see from the situation in the USA: new technologies are changing the nature of work itself.

Future jobs will not be the same jobs as in the past. In our country we must tailor education and create jobs in areas unaffected by globalization (competition, technology, low costs etc.), otherwise businesses will invest where there are global advantages and talent will go where the jobs are, which will cause a rupture between demand and job offers and salaries. The next "Minister of Employment" must look to investments that will create advantages for our country, without demagogy or defending other interests, especially in education, training, technology and infrastructure. But first it must be decided which sectors of our economy must be supported, like education, health, food, tourism, small and medium-sized businesses, etc.

309

Without a real plan for economic development, every kind of incentive will have subjective and limited effects. We must not forget that the businesses which earn the most in our country are those that export, and are worth 40% of the total: they have no problems taking on staff, and do so if need be. Those that are having problems (the other 60%) are those serving the domestic market, where demand is at a standstill. How can they be encouraged to hire staff if they are at 60% production capacity and there is no demand? The result lies in developing demand in the domestic market.

310

Globalization has killed off many previously economically important industrial groups, and has changed the role and power of banks. It has cancelled out ideological political parties and invented many other "technical" types, etc. Above all, at the local level strong groups have been killed off. We must prepare for more or less hostile takeovers, some less obvious than others, by the powers that govern the new global capitalism. But we should reflect: things being as they are, is this a good or a bad thing?

311

Reading the life of Bl. Giuseppe Toniolo gives us some idea of the times in which his thoughts, experiences and decisions took place. This era was shaped by terrible post-Napoleonic anti-clericalism. It was a time before and during the Risorgimento, which in the beginning also had the support of a large part of the Catholic world (e.g. Rosmini), before it became even more secular and statist. This was also a period of great grace, with the visions of the Virgin Mary at La Salette (1846), Lourdes (1858) and Fatima (1917). During Toniolo's lifetime (1846-1918), 123 apparitions of the Mother of God were recognized. In his apostolate on earth, Toniolo was assisted by Our Mother.

312

Giuseppe Toniolo was convinced that "if we (Catholics) are not like yeast, we are useless...," and he was thus not only exemplary but even courageous and heroic, even in a physical sense. Looking at the times in which he lived, we can understand what it was to be "heroic" and clash with the dominant "culture." It suffices to remember the attempt (during the pontificate of Leo XIII) to throw the body of Pius IX into the Tiber, or the monument to Giordano Bruno erected in the Campo de' Fiori. Toniolo was one of the few courageous men who did not fear the anti-clerical climate and instead became a leader, launching the Catholic Program against secular socialism (from which Murri drew inspiration for the Christian Democrats). Imagine what it would have meant at that time to combat the *Communist Manifesto* with the cry: "Working classes of the world unite... in Christ!"

313

Giuseppe Toniolo, in addition to being a man of great faith, was a man of study, organization and innovative ideas. He knew that strong actions require strong ideas and education, and re-launched neo-Thomistic studies at the university. Knowing that suitable tools are needed for action, he founded agricultural and credit co-operatives. He made plans for anti-statist corporations (as Don Luigi Sturzo did). Knowing that innovative ideas have to be in tune with the times, he reformulated the principles of the Church's social doctrine, and in doing this made it clear that the economy is merely a means; that man's behavior (and not the means) is ethical; that the whole point of economics is seeking the common good; that each economic decision is based on moral principles and has moral effects. He helped write Leo XIII's *Rerum Novarum*. He was a great, exemplary Catholic.

314

Pope John Paul II (in *Sollicitudo Rei Socialis*) and his successor Benedict XVI (in *Caritas in Veritate*) were right when they understood and predicted that modern man, whose technological and scientific capacities have grown rapidly but who still lacks the wisdom necessary to use them well, will be unable to control them, and this will lead to trouble. It is true that these instruments have escaped our control, and have even taken on (moral) autonomy, explaining or determining ideas and behaviors and limiting our ability to distinguish ends from means, both in economics and in other fields.

Just looking at economics, I would like to explain what has escaped modern man's control. Let us start with two facts. First, in deciding to ignore the intrinsic and sacred value of human life and, consequently, of the natural law, man has lost sight of the essential importance of children as he adapts and regulates economic laws. This has undermined the laws of economic growth, and with the creativity typical of the sinner who denies God and His laws, he wishes to promote his own laws. In the erudite and wealthy Western world's current crisis, growth based solely on individual consumption has taken the place of economic development based on a harmonious increase in population. The second is that since man ignores the uniqueness of his life, made up of flesh and spirit, the very logic and dynamism of economic development, in such a way that it is not undertaken in all facets of human life but only in the material aspect, has slipped from his grasp. This economic development is for the use and consumption of man as an "intelligent animal" who can be satisfied only materially by what he consumes. The GNP has been able to grow due to this attitude, with man upsetting the balance of the world economy, paving the way for a new world economic order, which will not only be economic but also cultural and spiritual, and could become the greatest revolution in the history of humanity.

315

At this point, after having lost control of the key laws of economics, man has lost control of many other things as well, to name just a few: control of inflation and deflation; control of public and private debt as well as interest rates; control of production and therefore of employment and unemployment; control of prices and resources, especially of raw materials; control of taxes necessary to sustain the costs of an artificially aging population; control of the production of wealth by companies which don't do market research and business plans; control of the production of wealth by private individuals and families, therefore lessening the amount of money put into savings; and control of consumption itself, as it is impossible to control the supply and demand of goods and purchasing power. The possibility of correcting these errors with moves to reduce the debt, kick-start the economy and establish a satisfactory economic balance has also vanished; the right types of politics and the necessary government, both between countries and within individual countries, to make coherent economic decisions, also seem to have vanished.

316

Let us reflect again on how this could have happened. Pope Benedict XVI explains in the introduction to *Caritas in Veritate* that it is because man has forgotten the meaning of life and of his actions. The dominant nihilism, the main philosophy of this age, has distanced man from truth, and without this truth he loses control of the instruments. How can you expect a banker to respect the meaning of his work (the real meaning, that it is geared toward the common good), if he is ignorant of life's meaning? How can you expect it of a scientist or politician, if his life has no meaning? If life has no meaning, why should human actions have meaning? Such people will probably have some opportunistic logic, influenced by the dominant way of thinking, that will point to what is fitting, what is good or evil, at any given moment in history. Why has this happened? I will offer a hypothesis that many lukewarm readers will balk at: it has happened because we have lost our connection with Christ, with God, because we no longer contemplate Christ and the meaning of creation, and therefore of our own lives. We have lost the drive and the will to imitate Christ and to be perfect like Him by living out our faith in Him with conviction, whether our job is banker, industrialist, politician, scientist, doctor, history teacher, etc.

317

Paradoxically (but not too much so), it is only by rediscovering these lost links that we can find solutions to this economic crisis that will be truly sustainable and opportune. I will say something that will shock some people: we will not be able to find and apply true solutions if the criteria we use are influenced by sin, and if we do not recognize the nefarious power of sin on our behavior, reflections and decisions as human beings.

Let's go back to sin and talk about how it influences human thoughts and actions. Every proposed solution to this crisis will be fleeting if it is influenced by the confusion that favors sin and denies the existence of sin and its consequences. Every plan influenced by pride, vanity, concupiscence, etc. will become unsustainable, because it ignores people's real needs in relation to their vocation to eternity and their need to become holy here on earth.

Paradoxically, nobody wants to consider a period of austerity as a way to restore the fundamentals of our economy, saying that individuals will be penalized; perhaps this austerity would penalize the popularity of those making the decision. But what if austerity really were the right solution, the best for individuals? If it is faith that gives us understanding of the mysteries of Christ, how can faith not help us understand possible and real solutions (which would naturally be technological) to an economic crisis? Without this faith, oft-mentioned expressions such as the "priority of the centrality of the person" have no meaning, to say nothing of electoral significance. What does the centrality of the person mean to an economist, a politician, or a scientist? Is it, at worst, seeing the person as a means of production, consumption and saving, or at best, recognizing the passing nature of possessions? Detachment from goods? The fragility of human life thanks to our passions?

Common sense is enough to realize all this; faith is not necessary. Any good philosopher without faith can explain why this is true, as these truths are found in natural laws we can all observe. Good economics is founded on natural laws useful for man, but an economy for man, for the person, requires a lot more: it requires consciousness of the dignity of man as a creature of God, child of God, heir of God. This is why I believe we need good priests rather than good economics teachers to have this good economy: priests who recognize and help us to hate sin. The economic miracle lies not in managing to overcome all the problems quickly so everyone can be rich again: it lies in accepting this (unpleasant) crisis as a means to gain real "wealth" which lasts longer, eternally.

Is it really true that Italy is weaker than other Western countries, or is it equally weak but in a different way? Let us begin by revisiting the problem of our debt, analyzing its growth and how it happened. The Italian public debt at the start of the crisis (2007) until 2009 rose by 14%, as it did in Germany, but less than in other European countries: Spain 28%, Ireland 50%, Portugal 19%, Greece 23%, the UK 36%; but it increased far less than in Japan, where it was 41%, and than in the USA, where it rose by 30% (source: IMF). Can we say we have been rigorous? The IMF forecasts that this public debt, as a percentage of GNP, will rise by 6% from 2010-2014 (from 118% to 124%), one more point than in Germany (5%) but less than in France (9%), the UK (11%), the USA (14%) and Japan (18%). I conclude that if these data are to be believed, Italy is one of the most virtuous countries, in spite of its difficulties.

319

The debt of a country is made up of four parts: public debt, private family debt, financial institutional debt, and industrial/commercial/service etc. debt. If we analyze Italy's debt as opposed to other countries' debt, we will discover that the Italian situation is different and should be better understood in order to make decisions. Total debt including all of the above-mentioned four kinds, and seen as a percentage of the GNP, finds Germany as the most virtuous (284%), then the USA, before the 2010 growth in public debt when private debt was nationalized (288% of GNP, rising to 400% after 2010), then Italy (321%), followed by France (330%), Spain (372%), the UK (406%, rising to 484% when considered as a global banking hub). In reality, each country has its own problems; each has forced up one of the four components of the debt, and each has a specific "sensitivity" to *deleveraging* (debt reduction).

320

Just as positive rights are based on natural rights, so economic laws are based on natural laws, which we cannot evade. I ask two simple questions: 1. How can true economic growth, GDP growth, happen if the population does not grow? 2. How can the population grow in such a way that it benefits the whole of society?

321

The answer to the first question is the following: if the population does not grow, then after a few alternative corrective efforts, economic growth comes about through higher pro capita consumption. These alternatives to population growth include higher productivity of the economic system (which in fact means labor-saving investments) which reduces costs and permits greater consumption. But in the global market it is rather difficult. Then there is the exportation of production to countries where labor costs are (temporarily) less, resulting in more cheap imports which (temporarily) increase purchasing power and consumption.

Once these two solutions are exhausted, consumption grows only if people stop saving and go into debt, in the hope that their future income will cover this. The unforeseen problem that spoils everything for those who think having lots of children means greater poverty instead of greater wealth, is that when there are fewer births, social structures change, with the population getting older and becoming more costly (health, pensions…). To absorb these costs, consumption has to be increased, which leads to debt. But since this is not enough, taxes go up, which reduces spending and investment power. This is the problem of the family. Why is it that even though today both husbands and wives work, a family's true spending power is less than 25 years ago, when only the husband worked and the wife could stay at home to look after the children without worrying about the future? This is because, in those 25 years, taxes as a percentage of the GNP have doubled, from about 25% in 1980 to about 48% in 2005, to about 50% in 2010. In practice, this has halved income (and thanks to the euro it has become even worse), so people are not confident about starting families and having children. Paradoxically, not having children in the last thirty years makes it more difficult to have them (and to want to have them) today.

322

The answer to the second question is this: the family is the real "engine" of economic growth because it creates reasons and stimuli for investing, consuming and saving. Children are not only born but also educated, to the benefit of society. I believe that today we need to be "re-educated" concerning the value of the family. This would require a concerted effort and a strong, non-nihilistic way of thinking.

323

I believe that the real educational role of the Church and her institutions throughout the world is not well enough known. I believe that if the Church's institutions were to disappear from the social sphere, public expenditure would have to rise considerably, but without the results that only love for one's neighbor can give. The Church gives man four kinds of "nourishment:" the first is spiritual (the sacraments); the second is intellectual (doctrine); the third is moral (hope); and the fourth is corporal: from the practical charity of feeding the hungry to assisting and caring for to the poor, the sick and the lonely. The manual that tells us how to understand and overcome this economic (and moral) crisis is Benedict XVI's encyclical *Caritas in Veritate*, which I urge all to read and reflect upon.

324

I am convinced through reflection and experience that economics is not a true and proper science. A cause does not produce an effect if many factors enter in, distorting the context. The neo-Malthusian theses are proof of this. A socio-economic anti-child culture has been peddled so people can become wealthier, and the result is that we have become poorer.

325

In Catholic morals, the economic problem is substantially linked to human dignity. In antiquity the working man was a slave. Christianity imposed the equality of all, since all are God's children. In the sixth century, Benedictine monasteries transformed work into a way of progress for man, showing man its significance and meaning.

After the discovery of America, philosophical thought, natural law and economic thought changed (cf. the School of Salamanca). The Reformation "corrupted" the sense of sin and the meaning of human acts. The Enlightenment and physiocracy paved the way for the Industrial Revolution when the work-capital relationship changed. Marxism made it a tool of struggle. Utilitarianism tried to give Marx's definition of work a new meaning, but the economy did not improve. Keynes made it a political instrument. Globalization split the world in two, and man into three. This shows us the need for a new economic policy that can reconcile man into a single dimension. Who will do this? I tried, but they got rid of me… It is more difficult to do good than evil in a world corrupted in its very spirit.

326

Before facing the logic of a proposal linked to social doctrine, it is opportune to remember the history of the Roman Question, the link between the Church's temporal and spiritual power, and thus her credibility in economic matters. The problem of the means at the Church's disposal goes back to the first centuries after Christ (Clement of Alexandria). Let us leave aside the economic aspects of the Reformation, especially those of Henry VIII of England. In 1807 Napoleon finally succeeded in invading the Papal States and suppressing their temporal power. The Congress of Vienna (1815) restored it. During the Risorgimento, after defeating the Austrians (1859) and proclaiming Rome the capital of Italy, the Church's temporal power was liquidated ("A free Church in a free state"), but Pius IX refused to accept this and issued a condemnation (his 1864 Syllabus). This dispossession, however, remains theoretical. Leo XIII (1878) confirmed it [the condemnation?] *(Rerum Novarum,* 1891). Pius X (1903-1914) reconfirmed it. Pius XI (1929) signed the Lateran Treaty (to avoid the worst).

327

Social doctrine was born during the years when the Church's temporal power was under attack and she was accused of every sort of crime as an excuse to strip her of it. The main accusation was that she used the means at her disposal badly, and performed works of spiritual charity rather than of material charity (which became considered "social justice"). Social doctrine is founded on the meaning of human life; it distinguishes between ends and means; it considers the economy a tool that should be used for the benefit of man, who is a child of God.

This social doctrine was never accepted by secularism due to the latter's key principles: that human life has no meaning, and that man was not created by God. (For them), what does explain man is the theory of evolution, and science is what explains "the work of God." This demonstrates the impossibility of reconciling Catholicism and secularism regarding the role of the economy for man. And yet, Einaudi proposed a "third way" between socialism and capitalism, which would guarantee individual liberty and the necessary subsidiarity. It was never applied or taken seriously for various reasons, the first of which was that people would have to listen to the Church's Magisterium; the second, it would require the State to be hands-off in economics; the third is that the Church [supposedly] has no right to play a part in economics, which should have moral autonomy. This moral autonomy is the origin of the current crisis.

328

It is encouraging to hear people hope that the Church, as a recognized international moral authority, would give her opinion on social or individual moral behavior, but it would be even more encouraging if the Church were encouraged to teach the principles behind this behavior!

329

Often attempts to remind people of moral principles, to teach them and use them as a guide, have not been so encouraged. Often they have been derided as false and artificial, which has given comfort to a certain culture that considers a moral life only as a "mask" which hides real life. If this were true, it would mean that human life has a split personality. This illness can only be treated by special "doctors": good priests, but they should not cure this disease with the pleasing sort of medicine that makes excuses for human behavior, or they will be guilty of a sin of omission: neglecting to give appropriate spiritual care. When this omission has taken place, it has allowed various caricature-like forms of morality to take root in common culture. In reality, human life has suffered and still suffers from one disease: rejection of God and separation from Him; so the cure must be fitting and sufficient.

330

When the moral authority expresses deep suffering on seeing the decadence in customs stemming from separation from God, this is mainly due to his knowledge that man needs help—real, loving help. This help, in order to reinforce man's moral vision, starts with teaching the supernatural meaning of life and consequently of human actions. This is what is needed to reestablish private and public morals, in complete unity of life, indispensable to the maturation of society which all would like to see. The encyclical *Caritas in Veritate* is a good "how-to" manual for this.

331

People often wonder what the real economic value of the family is. An economic value is never intrinsic (e.g. diamonds in Africa) but is influenced by a context of civilization and its maturity and customs. A society needs to have an IDENTITY, with ends and aims in order to realize its natural vocation; otherwise this vocation will be carried out in a disorderly, reckless, irresponsible and unproductive way. The family is central to this process. A society without the family structure can have children, but without creating values of education and love (for their parents and those around them). Without the family structure a socially and economically disorganized society is created, because it is the family that produces sustainable well-being (production-savings-investment-consumption). Therefore if it were true that Christianity invented the family, this would be enough to award Christianity the Nobel Prize in economics.

332

How much is the family worth from an economic point of view? The answer is complex: how much is an "educated" person's contribution to society worth? How much is the family's system of protecting its own (children, the elderly, the sick) worth? How much is the family's production system worth?

333

Today there are still those who preach about keeping the birth rate down to help the economy recover... Today there are still those who explain that the family is an invention of priests, which creates selfishness and non-egalitarian societies through a subjective and particular means of education. There are still those today who want a state education system based on knowing-how instead of knowing-why. It must be remembered that denigrating the family not only breaks natural social and economic relationships, but also prevents children from being brought up by a father and a mother, a husband and wife united in the sacrament of matrimony for whom morals count. Denigrating the family hinders real, sustainable economic growth and instead leads to more taxes. It hinders the creation of real jobs, especially domestically. Naturally it does not allow for new marriages... and children. But it also renders the care of the elderly more difficult, due to a lack of resources (consequently leading to euthanasia?). Perhaps I already said this before, but Cain was against the family too and was in favor of birth control. He was the first...

334

It would be good if environmentalists and climate-change experts reflected on who is to blame, and for what. The nihilistic way of thinking that rejects all values and objective truths, applied to economics, costs humankind dearly thanks to the errors it spawns. Think of the disastrous consequences of the Malthusian theories founded on the prejudiced opinion that population growth creates misery. Think of the consequences of applying utilitarian doctrines which, in separating economic values from intrinsic values, have led to the collapse of the realistic structure of the economy. Think of the consequences of applying the economy's supposed moral autonomy, which in confusing ends with means (i.e. profit) and promoting economic relativism has meant that only the tangible is valued, and has caused the consumerist and materialistic behavior we so lament. We could go on and on.

335

Concerning environmental problems, those who espouse the nihilistic way of thinking are producing even greater damage. First they tried to convince man that he was an "intelligent" animal and could do as he wished without any rules, driving to the max his selfishness and seeking only what is useful: power, pleasure and oppression; then they tried to demolish the conviction that life has meaning and that human actions consequently have some meaning; now they claim that the confusing effects of climate change can be solved by reducing the birth rate and deindustrializing, instead of appreciating the values which would return man to his original dignity. This strategic vision of the problem is missing because the spread of nihilistic thought leads man to believe in nothing, and as a consequence, to believe that human life has no value or meaning in itself, but rather that Nature, which man damages by his actions, is at the center of things. In not seeking, and indeed denying, the truth, how can the global economy, and thus the environment, be governed? This nihilistic thought risks transforming the best form of globalization for poor countries into a state of disorder, which will be blamed on the global economy as well as on man, who is the origin of environmental damage and therefore worthy of self-elimination.

336

Blaise Pascal wrote: "There are no doubt natural laws, but fair reason once corrupted has corrupted all." It also seems to have corrupted the ability to objectively evaluate the global economy, modern technology and economic freedom. These are all means that, in the hands of the selfish and individualistic "intelligent animal," lead to abuse.

337

Environmentalists are right in drawing attention to the misused (by many) environment, but these ecologists would do better to read the encyclical *Caritas in Veritate*: they would understand better why, how, and for whom the environment should be respected. (If that happened, however, we would have to acknowledge that this would be the end of nihilistic thought and thus of the "death of God" theology which turns into death for man.)

338

Paul VI's *Humanae Vitae* was very clear on the subject: in rejecting life (births) there is the risk that death will be imposed on the unproductive, superfluous, costly and no longer economically sustainable elderly. Since the elderly are statistically becoming the majority, and they vote, they form a consistent and dangerous electoral group. So the suppression of the elderly has to happen by their own choice, an autonomous and free decision taken when they feel unworthy to live, when they feel they are useless and harmful burdens for the young. To get to this decision, the psychological conditioning has to be perfect.

This is quite different from euthanasia, which considers giving a suffering person a "good death" an act of mercy. No, choosing to die voluntarily is much worse: it is the rejection of life and its sacredness, and then, even worse, suicide deprives those who choose it not only of earthly life but also of eternal life. These concepts are expressed well in a booklet written in 1978 by the Swedish intellectual Carl H. Wijkmark *(Modern Death)* and published in Italian in 2008 by Iperborea. In this booklet the author imagines a bioethics congress and what rational men of science discuss there.

339

[In this booklet], the context is real and the demographic problem has now exploded. Abortion is rampant, and childless young people coexist with a population that has aged, partly due to medical progress. There is now an incurable economic imbalance. The elderly are not only expensive to support, but in addition, they cannot even produce anything or maintain themselves by working, because the collapse of development (and of work) due to the demographic collapse, prevents this. For these reasons, the problem should be solved with their collaboration, not by acting against them.

The question then becomes: how can the elderly who are neither terminally ill nor suffering be convinced to ask for euthanasia? The merit of this booklet, mentioned in point 339, is that it foresaw the factors we are already imagining today. If man is merely an intelligent animal with all the dignity of an evolved bacterium, we should not be surprised if these bioethical hypotheses soon become reality. All the ingredients are there, and the writer has been trying to explain this for years, but no one is listening.

I had not imagined this hypothetical solution and I think it is a great one, in a demonic sense. We are not far from a new ethics of life and death where evil will be presented as good. A decision to commit suicide is taken out of respect for the (socio-economic) value of the lives of others. Here is the greatness of evil: to appear good. Here is the greatness of relativism and nihilism: to consider the sacredness of human life according to the available economic means.

This is evident if ethics are relative to time and space. Relative ethics teach that there are too many old people to support, so they should be gotten rid of for the good of humanity. Thus new socio-economic ethics influences or dulls individual conscience in favor of public conscience. New relativistic bioethics is getting ready to make great leaps forward after resolving anthropological questions, denying the origin of man as a creature. It can do this by denying natural law, accepting "natural selection," confusing ends with means, etc., perhaps with the help of some moral authority that accepts the concept of greater common good being superior to the private good, and accepts a private conscience free of superstition and selfish hypocrisy. Thus selfishness could become the real sin, more so than absolute respect for human life, if people come to fear the risks of poverty, hunger and misery. Think of a typical announcement based on these premises: "How many lives could be saved if we did not have to support the elderly…"

340

For many years I have tried to explain both theoretically and technically that the fall in birth rate means it is impossible to sustain the costs of the elderly who have left the productive cycle, and that the solution lies in the birth rate returning to a natural rate without the neo-Malthusian influences of the 1970s. How often I have tried to explain that birth control leads to controlling death as well, but this was taboo. Facing the problem, following papal teachings and Church Magisterium, have cost me dearly... Can we expect a new encyclical on the value of life and death? One that reminds us that death is the gate to eternal life?

341

A few years ago the former Italian President Francesco Cossiga gave me a little red book which he had had printed out of devotion to J.H. Newman: *Newman's Book of Prayers*. In the introductory biography of J.H. Newman (1801-1890) we read of the anxiety he felt in his life, of his search for true conversion. Prayer and study, harmoniously transforming study into prayer and prayer into a study of God's will, aided this search. Thus it was that Newman concluded that the Roman (Roman!) Catholic Church was "Christ's only flock." The biography also states that Newman claimed loyalty to the Anglican Church while defending the Roman Church (*Apologia Pro Vita Sua*, 1864). Newman can therefore reasonably be considered a protector of those non-Catholics converting to Catholicism. The prayers in the book are wonderful examples of how to address the Father and why: like a child, above all, who asks to reach perfection by doing what God wants, conscious of his unique personal responsibility (prayer, 4th day); conscious that proclaiming the Lord is done through example and personal actions (prayer, 8th day). But the prayer for Church unity (18th day) deserves to be printed here in full and meditated on, especially in these times: "Lord Jesus Christ, who when You were about to suffer, did pray for Your disciples to the end of time that they might all be one, as You are in the Father, and the Father in You: remove the barriers that separate Christians of various denominations; teach all that the See of Peter, the Holy Church of

Rome, is the foundation, the center and the instrument of this unity; open their hearts to the long-forgotten truth that our Holy Father the Pope is Your Vicar and Representative, so that, as there is in heaven only one holy company, so likewise there may be one communion, confessing and glorifying Your Holy Name here below."

Newton prayed as a man conscious of his personal responsibility in having to fight and suffer in the world without becoming of the world, in order to find the way to eternal salvation. His prayers invite us to seek the meaning of life and of our actions, with personal responsibility. These are essential factors in reconstructing man today.

342

I shall try to explain why work is one of the most important problems we face today. There are three reasons. The first is that work is changing; the second is that the model of economic development will soon change, if it has not done so already; and the third is that labor organizations will be forced to adapt to these previous two factors, and they are already consciously doing so.

343

We see why work is changing. When the wealthy and developed world, concerned about a population explosion, decides to encourage birth control, it sets in motion two processes aimed at increasing the GNP without increasing the population: higher productivity (which means technology) and exportation of production (to increase purchasing power). These factors lead to higher consumption and debt, producing an acceleration of the aforementioned two processes, in the hope of compensating for the growth of debt in order to finance consumption, to compensate for the growth of fixed costs caused by an aging population (and the consequent growth in necessary taxes), and to compensate for the depletion of savings which have been sacrificed to this consumerism. The process of accelerated globalization delocalizes production, exporting it to countries with low-cost labor, creating job opportunities there but the risk of unemployment here.

This has obviously not been well thought through. An economic crisis, which explodes when the debt necessary to support consumption (which in turn is necessary for growth) becomes unsustainable, leads to a collapse in consumption, wealth, production, employment and the consequences that we now see. After the crisis following this accelerated process of globalization, it is very difficult to return to nearly full employment in developed countries, as what will make these formerly rich countries competitive again are technological solutions (which reduce job numbers), savings, and reducing waste (which in the end means jobs).

344

Let us look at the problem of work. Technology changes the nature of work and creates differences between employment supply and demand, both locally and especially globally, mostly thanks to job exporting and industrial changes that have modified the demand for work and its quality, with a resulting impact on income, purchasing power, consumption and growth. In the last ten years, millions of jobs that are susceptible to competition (exported labor, technology) have been lost in the West, and jobs have been created (in healthcare, civil service, education…) only in those areas which are not exposed to global competition but which produce a much lower GNP.

What counts is that jobs created for the future are no longer those created in the past. The immediate consequence is the level of education schools can give and the demand for jobs produced by this change. This means that employment must be changed, by investing in order to create new capacities, but these will have much lower remuneration in terms of GNP. It is obvious that, regardless of age group, salaries will be influenced by the country's new capacities for growth or by its economic decline. Given the delay in the Western world's acknowledging that past growth rates were unsustainable, the reaction (e.g. investing in education, technology, infrastructure) cannot be immediate, as both capital and a long period of time are necessary for results to be seen.

In the meantime, our world, wanting to tackle the job problem (which cannot be resolved through moralistic or demagogic admonishments), needs to solve a series of contradictions: more or less state investment? More consumption or more savings to sustain growth and the monetary base? More protectionism or a greater market to sustain employment? Greater efficiency or more jobs? More taxes for public expenditure or more resources for consumption and investment? More immigration or more children? And so on. The fact is that we seem oblivious to the fact that we have created a new economic order whose dynamic, especially regarding work, we have trouble understanding; so much so that some say every crisis is an opportunity! Certainly, if man were wise and could distinguish between ends and means, every crisis would be an opportunity. But if, as Benedict XVI says in the introduction to *Caritas in Veritate*, there is a rampant nihilistic culture, a crisis remains a crisis and produces others. The sophisticated tool has slipped out of immature man's grasp… Man needs to change, and holy priests who can effect this change are needed. We must pray that God will grant us the necessary shepherds.

345a

In the encyclical *Caritas in Veritate*, Benedict XVI makes a fundamental reflection concerning migration (Chapter 5, paragraph 62): he explains that it is a complex phenomenon that cannot easily be solved by any country, but he reminds us that each migrant is a human being with rights. Bearing this in mind means recognizing the dignity of each human being, no matter who he or she is. This acknowledgement implicitly requires a certain moral vision that does not see a person, here specifically a migrant, as a means of production, contribution or consumption, but as an end.

With this in mind, we must now ask ourselves why this problem of immigration exists. We Italians have been doing this for over twenty years, since about the same time as the birth rate started falling in the 1980s, and the question remains due to the nearly ten-fold rise in the number of legal immigrants in that period (from just over 500,000 in 1990 to 4,500,000 in 2009; 50% of these are from inside the EU and 50% from outside), meaning that they make up over 8% of the Italian population. In all this time, Italy has shown itself to be one of the countries most willing to offer asylum or humanitarian protection, and so I refute any accusations of racism or xenophobia.

345b

It is true that there are various categories of migration. One kind is desirable, due to a need for laborers. There is also the involuntary kind that, however, is due to solidarity and is humanitarian; it can be illegal or clandestine; it can be like the Chinese model in which a country expands and exports its production activities and population. It is obvious that the current phenomenon of migration coincides with two main factors: the competitive needs of different economic areas due to globalization, and (as a consequence) the need to support a population whose birth rate is falling (as in the case of European countries, specifically Italy).

These two phenomena confound the origin of these migration processes, seeing the immigrant of whatever type as a useful means of production and contribution. No doubt, this has given many people at least a minimum standard of living, considering the small but real fiscal contributions generated by the activity of four million immigrants, but we must reflect on the level of immigration necessary to make up for the unwillingness of the domestic workforce to take "menial" jobs. Costs aside, the immediate objection is whether it is good to allow those who do not wish to do this type of work to be supported by welfare checks. But perhaps the real problem is that these jobs should be made more financially attractive, as our country has high living costs. Immigrants take low-level jobs because they accept the unjust and precarious standard of living this type of work brings. We see the paradox of both unemployment and immigration rising at the same time, without creating better standards of living: this risks aggravating unemployment and ill-feeling if the present crisis continues, even in wealthier regions where immigrants have found work. The problem is really complex and not easily solved.

345c

I believe that, with exceptions for specific cases and humanitarian reasons, the best thing an immigrant can do is to sustain economic development in his own country, as he is one of its precious resources. A Marshall Plan for the poorest countries would be a solution to the crisis, which we have been suggesting for a couple of years and has been accepted as worthwhile by politicians. If this solution is not enacted, because we think it is better to compensate our falling birth rate with increased immigration, then, in addition to the humanitarian reasons listed above, we should take a good look at the economic calculations involved. We are too used to seeing forecasts and economic plans, which affect the person, be unsustainable and damaging to man.

346

There is no doubt that good and opportune economic laws exist: these are the laws of natural economics. Nature is orderly, not the fruit of chaos. But human reason, which has been progressively corrupted, is even more corrupted than its own nature and has corrupted the use of these laws. Sometimes hearing continual calls for more morality in economics becomes unbearable: which morals are being talked about? Natural morals referring to religious teaching, or those generated arbitrarily and freely by man's ungoverned instincts with no absolute reference points?

347

Freedom is a means that presupposes the recognition of a natural end and is pursued within the accepted boundaries of these natural obligations. In practice, freedom is not an end in itself, but is subordinate to a precise aim: the common good. Instead, economic freedom is understood as an end in itself, which produces human values. In other words, the materially satisfied man is real morality.

Is this true? Is the free man moral? Or is the moral man free? If it is true that we really possess only what we can do without (otherwise it would be those things which possess us), it is the tyranny of material goods which man today sees as freedom. True freedom of choice presupposes detachment from the non-essential, where not having it is equal to having it, because it either has a useful end or it is irrelevant, useless and superfluous.

348

The man who knows what morals are does not fear economic rationality; he fears the misuse of economic instruments. This misuse of economics arises when man loses his way and loses the truth. After getting his objectives wrong, he gets strategic choices wrong as well. To give an example from the social arena, if he gets the objective of defending the weakest wrong, he also misuses the instrument (e.g. state assistance). In politics, to reach the objective of equality and brotherhood, one can err by pursuing this end with irrational egalitarianism. In art, it can go as far as producing incomprehensible, formless objects which adorn homes and art collections, but represent nothing at all; the official explanation is that they represent nothing, or perhaps the ridiculous, but it is a ridiculous nothing, often very expensive and thus suspect... where the true artist turns out to be the critic who explains these works and makes people appreciate them. It is not the first time in history that a culture has had to wonder whether to renew itself or disappear.

349

Civilizations are mortal, since man creates and destroys them himself. Man maintains his dominion over nature; he can destroy and rebuild everything and writes the history that follows, so is it not true that we should learn from history? But from which history? Written by whom? The problem arises and grows when spiritual heresies are created which undermine nature (Descartes' pure reason vs. practical reason), and break the unity of life. The Cartesian precept of division between reason and practice has confused (some would say destroyed) man, because man needs this unity of natural life. When body and soul are distinguished and separated from each other, it impedes the functioning of both because it leads reason to seek the truth in itself, and the will no longer seeks both the material and spiritual good, but only material satisfaction. Thus civilization is no longer a development of the values embodied in human nature, but a confused exploitation of disposable resources that results in an incomplete development. In separating body and soul, the economy no longer satisfies man. In separating soul, body and intellect, the foundations are laid for absolute nihilism.

350

Today an abstract form of economic dogmatism, detached from reality, seems to have triumphed. This has led to confusion in how to understand the current economic crisis, whose causes can be seen in its effects. The causes are the fall in birth rate in the West (in practice for moral reasons), but the fault continues to be laid at the door of the misuse of instruments, capitalistic models, etc. We forget that instruments are neutral things in man's hands; he can choose to use them well or badly. If the diagnosis is wrong, how can the right remedy be found? Proudhom dreamed of being able to eliminate the bad side of things and to keep the good side: in the same way, there are some today who want to resolve the crisis by eliminating capitalism's bad side. But which side is that? As Benedict XVI explains in *Caritas in Veritate*, it is men rather than instruments who should be renewed.

351

How come finance governs the economy and even politics? Finance governs the economy when an economic system is deindustrialized, but this is not enough. Finance also governs the economy when an economic system's debt, accumulated to finance consumption for growth, exceeds real values and becomes unsustainable. Alongside this, finance governs the economy when there are no savings, which are the monetary base for creating credit, when savings are not created and are instead sacrificed to sustain the consumption necessary for growth. Then, banks expand credit on their capital for supervisory purposes, have to find derivatives and thus increase risk. In practice, finance governs the economy when there is too much debt and few savings.

352

This is not the complete explanation. Finance governs the economy even more when speculation and "bubbles" are relied on to make assets grow to guarantee debt, instead of productivity and income. It becomes even more important when stock or property values have to be sustained to guarantee this debt. The government of finance becomes ever more necessary if monetary expansion is used to resolve the crisis, but then the fear of inflation arises. It becomes an important instrument when a respected entrepreneur becomes an investment fund for others (substituting the traditional entrepreneur with the manager with his various stock options), managing the savings of institutions that must give returns. He cannot have a long-term vision but only a short-term one, and the results are evaluated in the very short term.

353

Finance begins governing the economy when the concept of "(future) value for the shareholder" becomes a slogan to attract capital. We see that finance rules when ratings agencies become referees of the economy, of values and of the truth. We see it even more when interest rates due to, let us say, *force majeure* (to sustain weak economies) are at zero, below the rate of inflation and cause imbalances and speculation (perhaps deliberately). It becomes so in a critical way when governments require a growth in GNP and have to sustain it or force it to absorb necessary expenses, not to mention necessary interventions of nationalization or rescue. In practice, finance governs politics more and more when it seeks to resolve problems without creating income and savings, and even more so when it causes a (speculative) rise in financial values (of either movable or fixed property) without real growth.

To have this credibility, finance must be officially recognized as a science, and financiers must be recognized as high priests who decide what is true. This happens when man gets confused and means become ends, and this situation triumphs when these means take on moral autonomy and the ends are no longer those of the common good. Finance governs the economy when there are no longer any real leaders who consider leadership as a means of pursuing the common good.

354

Moral authority aims to influence choices concerning marriage and procreation with the objective of helping those with a vocation to marriage find life's real meaning, with attention also paid to the economic aspects of the demographic problem. Today it is easier to imagine that demographic policies can be economic rather than moral, yet a pragmatic sense of responsibility can triumph over moral persuasion when it comes to encouraging people to have children, telling them it is the right thing to do instead of the "good" thing to do. Unfortunately, in a deep crisis of ideas and culture, it is easier to influence behavior than hope to influence ideas.

355

In thirty years only scant attention has been paid to the problem of the falling birth rate, despite the continual warnings in various papal encyclicals. In *Mater et Magistra* (Chapter 2, par 172 etc.), John XXIII prophetically predicted the problems that would explode just 15-20 years later thanks to the neo-Malthusian culture. There are the two extraordinary encyclicals by Paul VI (*Humanae Vitae* and *Populorum Progressio*), which became starting points for Benedict XVI's *Caritas in Veritate*, which is a true reference work for those who want to understand the link between economic laws and morality in globalization. The consequence of this lukewarm attention to papal warnings has been behavioral decadence, which in turn led to the economic problem of the falling birth rate in the Western world.

356

Sacrificing the birth rate has meant that consumption has had to increase (if the population does not increase, GNP will only grow if individual consumption rises), and the aging and increasingly costly population has become economically unsustainable, causing a proportionate rise in taxes on the GNP. This explains why, comparatively speaking, a couple today earns less than one head of the family did thirty years ago, and people complain that they cannot afford to get married and have children. Some have had the illusion, and still do, that they are financially better off without children. This is an unpardonable error. Without population growth, i.e., with no children in a mature economic system, real and sustainable economic growth collapses, and the resources to support the aging population are lacking. This implies that economic growth can be obtained by temporary means, greater consumption and less saving. In a mature socio-economic system, fewer births mean higher fixed costs and higher taxes (to absorb higher pension and health costs), increased debt in order to finance the necessary consumption, and the creation of greater risks. As a consequence, there is a lack of resources for creating more jobs (these jobs are moved abroad in order to import and consume at a lower cost) and the need arises to bring in immigrants. You will see that we will be forced to face this problem for economic reasons, with the risk that the culture of pragmatic responsibility will win over the culture of moral persuasion. Conditions for increasing the birth rate will be created (out of necessity), but conditions will also be created to accelerate the "sacrifice" of the "useless and expensive" elderly. The pragmatism of the culture of responsibility is a risk when culture is weakened and easily influenced. Support for the virtuous concept of forming families and having children must be stimulated politically, but moral reasons for this must be retaught, with an attitude of loving and raising children, as the elderly should also be loved and respected. It is then that we will start coming out of this structural moral crisis.

357

The CEO of Fiat, Sergio Marchionne, is right when he says we need to get serious. The situation is perhaps more dire than it seems. In so-called developed countries the natural progress of opulence has been interrupted, if indeed it is not at an end, as forecast by Adam Smith. The next few decades risk seeing only economic growth in emerging countries, thanks not only to low-cost production but also to new technology, with the creation of capital and capacity greater than the West can contain. This will transform emerging countries into high-consumption countries, attracting other productive investments traditionally found in the West; in the developed and formerly rich West, the risk is the occurrence of the opposite process.

358

Economics' "Law of Gravity" will mean investments are transferred more and more to the developing world, while fixed costs due to the aging population will become unsustainable, with the GNP in continual free-fall. In a world where ideas and knowledge circulate freely, the winners will be those who know how to transform these into competitive capacities. These are then transformed into lower costs, which is to consumers' advantage. However, the advantage to consumers can clash with the advantage to producers who do not have these competitive advantages, and so they risk having to lay off staff, causing unemployment and poverty. This is due to the fact that worldwide economic integration means the success of the cheapest products; more expensive producers fail, and the unchanging "human labor" productive factor is penalized, as this factor cannot be moved or changed at will.

It is on this problem that we must concentrate our "humanitarian" attention, yet due to a lack of other strategies, if we produce where labor is cheaper, employment is created there while unemployment is generated where costs are higher (think of this in the long term: where unemployment is created, lower salaries are accepted, creating new cost advantages; where employment is created, salaries and costs will both rise, and so on). With the exportation of production, aimed at obtaining cheaper products and higher purchasing power, developed countries have transferred work to developing countries. They have progressively modified the structure of their own economies, consuming more than producing, and encouraging growth in the GNP by means of debt. When this has become unsustainable, they have thrown in the towel, so states have intervened using public funds: greater GNP is required to sustain this, otherwise taxes on GNP become unsustainable.

359

How can we tackle these problems? We know it is easier said than done, but we should try just the same. They can be faced by increasing productivity (thanks to the advantages offered by technology and the digital economy), channeling savings into small- and medium-sized businesses thanks to the banking system, reviewing the European stability pact and devaluing the euro.

The growth in productivity of the Western worker is indispensable for this; let us say by 30-40% according to economic activities. This will imply a change in the mentality towards manual labor, which has to be reinvented more than guaranteed. Marchionne's suggestion should be seriously considered. Governments should pay attention to technological innovation and the digital economy, because this can strengthen our small and medium-sized businesses, create manual labor jobs and sustain a growth in GDP. I believe it is also necessary to reflect—despite the consequences of importing raw materials—on the need to offset the loss of competition by devaluing the euro and making exports of European products more attractive, which would mean the return of production and jobs to European countries.

There is often the impression that not everyone has understood what has happened to the global economy in the last thirty years and how this has worsened our situation. Many believe or hope that it will be the individual countries that try to solve their economic problems themselves, and this normally means that public debt rises. Some countries have done so and now regret it. Our country has not done this, thanks to a careful and judicious budgetary policy, but we still have savings and some extraordinary businessmen: these are important factors in "reinventing" work, even if they are not all that counts.

360

I like to think that the Parable of the Talents, if it were set in today's times, would include an extra character—the one who would invest his talent from the Lord in a high-risk, high-return financial product, instead of investing it wisely or even burying it. He would not only lose everything, but he would also damage his master's finances and reputation…

361

In his *Lectio Magistralis* given in Paris at a Cistercian abbey, Benedict XVI explained the essence of Catholic economics in a few key phrases: "God Himself is the Creator of the world, and creation is not yet finished. God works, *ergázetai*; thus human work is now seen as a special form of human resemblance to God, as a way in which man can and may share in God's activity as Creator of the world." Creation is not yet finished, and man can also participate in it by means of economic instruments, observing its specific laws, but recognizing that economics is only a means, and to make it function well, man must find its meaning. This in synthesis is the "Catholic model" of economics.

362

This original model (of when man worked with God) was corrupted, relativized even, confusing ends with means, using bad means to pursue good ends and in the end mystifying the very meaning of economic means, denying the natural laws of creation and the dignity of man as a creature of God. This happened at various times in history, which I want to talk about now.

363

The first and most important was the Protestant heresy, which produced (perhaps unintentionally) a selfish and unabashed form of capitalism, founded on faith without works and on the invitation to act without regard to virtue, which was looked upon as unattainable due to man's "corrupt nature" ("Sin all you want, but repent strongly"). As a consequence this Protestant capitalism inadvertently caused man's exploitation, the continuation of inequality, colonialism, wars…

364

The Protestant deformation of the economics was followed by other deformations, the first of which was the "physiocratic thought" centered on the need to recognize the "good government of nature" (and not the nature corrupted by sin), the consequence of which was total trust in the "economic man" to do as he pleased in the pursuit of his own private interests, which would lead to advantages for all (so-called *laissez-faire*): this was an indispensable concept for the

Industrial Revolution. The Enlightenment theory was that man was a "thinking animal" and held that the economy should only concentrate on satisfying his material needs, as his spiritual needs were merely an illusion. Let us not forget that this capitalistic Protestant-Enlightenment theory led to Marxism, which was followed (as reactions) by utilitarian economic models (which led to the real value of the economy being forgotten), and technocratic economic models (where technocrats are chosen to be the necessary new "high priests" of the socio-economic system), which have progressively separated economics from religion and increasingly endowed it with moral autonomy. Keynes considered economics absolute, stating that only science, not religion, could solve humanity's problems...

365

What has economics become in denying its roots in natural law and detaching itself ever more from Catholic morality, ignoring human dignity and needs? It has become a system in which means become ends, leading to the end of the ends and means themselves, as the current crisis, which we cannot handle, is showing us. Nobody is more convinced than I am that wealth must first be produced in order for it to be distributed, but the problem is "how" it is produced. Ignoring this question means relativizing the meaning of the economy.

366

Catholic morality does not impose on the market moral norms in place of economic laws. It does not hold that the free market acts against man only because demand is compromised by its weaknesses, and does not see materialism as an attack on values. Catholic morality sees the market and capitalism as a natural consequence of progress, and sees the need to reinforce man spiritually in order for him to be as mature spiritually as he is technically so that he can handle capitalism and the market... Economic relativism produces men who do not even know where to invest their talents and so destroy them. God works. Creation is still in progress, but are we co-operating in it or destroying it?

367

What "Western" man has lacked this century has been reason, which is the consequence of the certainty of man's nature as a creature of God. This is true reason. If Western man of today recognizes a certain gap between rich and poor, it is because he has been deprived of other "nutritive" factors, both intellectual and spiritual; he is only used to material factors. The disease which has corrupted human intelligence has been so successful because it has inclined man to consider himself as substantially an intelligent animal (?) to be satisfied by materially, through consumption. Now that the consumerist period is over, he is in debt, and now he discovers that the three facets proper to him, worker, consumer and saver-investor, were in conflict with one another. As he grew poorer, he discovered that there were others who were still rich, and he cried out at the injustice.

However, the real injustice had been there before: he had been deprived of the doctrine of the faith that kept man aware of his dignity as a child of God, which obliged him to observe the natural law—in economics too—which cannot be ignored. What has happened in recent times is none other than what Pope John Paul II foretold in *Sollicitudo Rei Socialis*, where he stated that a man of little wisdom would not be mature enough to handle the technological instruments he himself created, and that they would "slip from his grasp." This is exactly what has happened, and the reasons for these causes and the development of the consequences are perfectly analyzed and described by Benedict XVI in *Caritas in Veritate*. Have you all read it?

368

In Pope Francis' message to the World Economic Forum in Davos (17 January 2014), His Holiness exhorted those present first of all to reflect "on the causes of the economic crisis." This is because these are "moral" reasons, linked to a nihilistic culture that rejects moral values, rejects man's true dignity and leads him to seek only material satisfaction. This is a matter of life and death. If progress is only seen in material terms, the situation gets worse. Daily uncertainty is a consequence of the imbalance created by seeking only the material and ignoring the intellectual and spiritual.

When the technocrats, the high priests of our world, realized that it was no longer possible to circumvent reality, instead of recognizing their mistakes and changing course, they declared that they had failed and let the effects fall on those who had no means to fight back. Perhaps they even sought to draw some advantage from this course of action. They did all of this without asking anyone's forgiveness, and it is the weakest areas of the formerly rich Western world that are paying the price. They are the new poor, while the emerging countries have become just a little wealthier. Almost a third of the global population is much better off now than before, even though the problem of unequal distribution of wealth has to be faced there. This includes Africa, which in the next few years will experience undreamed-of economic growth.

369

Globalization, even if badly carried out, has produced its selfish "invisible" but nonetheless real "hand." In the Western world, some have certainly managed to benefit from the crisis itself. I think this is an abuse permitted by the system that has been created, and like all abuses it should be specifically punished. We must be careful, however, to distinguish between "rich producers" and "rich profiteers." It is useless and harmful to condemn "the rich" if they have created distributable wealth. In this economic phase, wealth has been distributed (perhaps unequally) internationally, from consumer nations (who no longer produce) to producer nations (who do not yet consume).

370

The injustice which has arisen, including in the economic field, concerns above all the distribution of spiritual values. The "non-distribution" of spiritual values has included the unawareness of man's dignity and of natural law in economics. Solving this crisis involves remaking man, not changing the instruments, as Benedict XVI explains in *Caritas in Veritate*. Faith must be shared, as well as the awareness that wealth must be created for man and according to natural law. Consequently, distributing this material wealth is both a moral and a real economic choice.

371

It would be apt if the next pontificate took inspiration from Thomism, which is more relevant today than ever before. It would be equally apt if the next Minister of Culture were inspired by Saint Thomas' doctrine proposing and defending the real value inherent in common sense, by which the people of today should be inspired. Thomism teaches governments to understand which needs must be most urgently satisfied, and how to produce for the true common good. Think of how this Thomistic solution could tackle this nihilistic disorder and the confusion produced as a consequence of materialism, inspired by naturalism, which has led to the economically and socially unproductive consumption of the current economic crisis.

372

Thomism is the key to reflecting on what to do, because it considers everything according to its nature and real being, and so it is a suitable model for solving every problem. Furthermore, Thomism considers intelligence as superior to will, in particular the intelligence of creation, from which follow the meaning of creation and the meaning of creatures' actions. If we creatures went back to seeking the (forgotten) meaning of life and actions, we would perform the miracle of "changing the world," not along Grillo's lines but along Saint Thomas': in a realistic, intelligent and logical way, and not along relativistic, hysterical and populist lines. From these principles we can intuit, or better, logically work out, what human freedom is, what man's true needs and satisfactions are, and what goals he ought to pursue—, the values which must inspire him, what are the important things, what is beautiful, and what is superfluous or to be avoided... In a word: "You shall know the truth, and the truth will set you free."

In practice, if we were sure we were God's creatures and bound to see Him after a demanding vacation spent on earth, how would we weigh our actions, ambitions and dreams? We doubt whether we are the fruit of creation: this is understandable, given our imperfections, so why don't we deepen our knowledge? I know this is not easy, due to the (dominant) culture in schools, and there is no help from philosophers or even priests, especially if the latter teach us relativism or that the truth comes from dialogue. Eve had a great dialogue with the serpent—and we see the results.

373

We must go back to being self-educated, choosing our teachers and understanding and rejecting lies and false ideals. We must learn to understand and renounce false ideas, but we can only do this by ourselves or with teachers we have chosen because we recognize that they want to teach us something, not for their own sake but for ours. As I understand it, man's knowledge and ideas are blank sheets; man is a blank in intelligence, in knowledge, in culture, in the capacity to receive and understand information, in the ability to decide and to act. We are our own worst enemies if we do not look to ourselves and our own real needs. Trying something new to resolve problems is barking up the wrong tree. Something real must be sought. Any politician can offer "something new," but only a wise person who believes in the laws of human nature can offer something really new, something eternal. Those who promise huge changes for the better while ignoring human nature and its unchangeable laws produce a series of banal novelties which end up destroying each other and wasting time and resources, leading to frustration and greater costs to re-establish the resulting imbalances.

374

The crazy politician makes promises for tomorrow, though he is ignorant of what the price will be, while the wise politician offers to do things at the right time and with the right actions, though of course with sacrifice. What religion offers, on condition of purifying the heart, the crazy revolutionary promises as a right without any responsibilities; later, he imposes sacrifice and unimaginable hardship on those ignorant of history and economics. The crazy revolutionary profits from expectations that neither politicians nor priests are able to fulfill. We must reflect on this. Exploiting man's delusional material expectations in order to set up a regime is inhumane. It is inhumane, just as it is inhumane to recognize in man only his material needs. Think of a political leader suggesting the "mortification" of the flesh, the nourishment of the intellect and the exaltation of the spirit: perhaps he is the one who loves you most. Perhaps he would also have to prepare you to understand and explain what this means, and why...

375

If you reread the introduction to *Caritas in Veritate*, you would understand why mankind is, or thinks it is, on the edge of a precipice that will soon give way. Is this happening because man is worse than he was before? No, it is because man has nourished himself on his own nature and has exhausted his natural reserves, as he no longer regenerates himself through repentance, confession and expiation. He has ruled out sin, and this has made man sterile: he does not feel the needs of the spirit or intellect, but only material needs. After filling our material needs to the saturation point and confusing our intellectual needs, how can we feel the need to rediscover the supernatural?

This is the real news: we need new heroes and new saints, otherwise how can we hope to solve current cultural, economic, and social problems, if not by returning to the Father's house like the prodigal son? But how can we speak of the supernatural to such a nihilistic world, without talking about philosophical concepts of the finite and the infinite, which nobody knows how to do anymore? Let us start with the definition of the supernatural: above what is natural, superior to creatures' capacities. The virtues that lead one to speak with God, to love Him and understand Him are supernatural; with divine grace, nature can be surpassed, but grace does not exist without nature, and cannot be separated from it. It is difficult now to find men who live by reason and think along the lines of grace and reason. When we say that man must change and learn to do things well and so on, we make a mistake: man today is sick and must recover, and this is not done just by speaking about mercy and charity.

376

We are facing problems that are greater than ourselves and our capabilities: think of moral problems concerning what is good and what is evil when cultures and laws, which must become uniform throughout the modern world, force us to think differently from how we (still) think. Moral authorities do not always help us understand what truth is, and are often ready to relativize it using sophistry and confusion. We must arm ourselves with an adequate rational process, keeping in mind that the rational and intelligent man, when faced with a problem, asks himself what his ideal objectives are in reference to the problem, and what impedes or conditions these aims, conforming the solution to these objectives.

Such a man, faced with a problem that is difficult or beyond his strength, could say that it is impossible to solve the problem. He could even compromise on the objective, or simply betray the objective. There is another possibility: he can tell himself that the objective was wrong and thus that the problem did not need solving, which denies the truth and does not respect ideals. This leads to a divorce between the real and the ideal, between the ability to understand and reach objectives and a virtuous vision of (the common) good. This signals the end of ideals and virtues, and is the triumph of evil. This also breaks up society and deprives it of true freedom, because freedom does not mean being independent of every thing, fact or person; real freedom consists in depending only on what one loves. One lacks freedom if he depends on what he does not love.

377

Sometimes we ask ourselves why and how Christianity, founded by Christ, has become corrupted, and by whom. Certainly, the agnostic-atheistic revolutionary who would wish to destroy it seems less dangerous than those who wish to prostitute it from the inside. As Benedict XVI said, men and natural law need to be reconstructed. If it is true that the divine passes through man, nature must be reeducated; this is what Benedict means by the educational emergency. Man must seek and find holiness on earth, because Heaven begins on earth itself. Benedict's realism comes from his belief in a holy materialism: sanctifying man on earth, protecting nature, reestablishing its laws, repairing and reforming. I believe that only the leaven of Christianity, through the actions of holy individuals, can change the world. The reconstruction of the social, political and economic order comes via individual conversion, and denying this is the greatest lie. It is a truly terrible thing to say that evil on earth lies in the errors of social organizations, but it is true that a "holy" society helps individuals sanctify themselves. Those who should have the greatest responsibility in leading man to the eternal Good prefer to camouflage the truth (and man himself), instead of seeking to change man by clearly explaining the truth to him.

378

We would like to have a society able to create well-being while remaining independent from money, substituting intellectual and spiritual values for financial ones. It is one thing to seek and offer alternatives to the excesses of a form of capitalism whose end (instead of its means) is to make profit for the few; it is another to want to destroy private capitalism in favor of state capitalism. Yet another is the non-capitalism we have seen in the last few decades, which has "invented" consumerism to counterbalance the ignorance of natural law, leading to a fall in the birth rate. This non-capitalism is more worrisome than the capitalism other states have proposed in the past. This is the capitalism of dissolution.

379

Let us look at the problem of the common good. I believe that men are indifferent to the true common good, perhaps because they do not know what it is and confuse it with people being well-off. Ever since man decided to do without God, everything has been a conflict, especially between man's will and his nature, between what is real and what is an illusion, between life and dissipation of life, between man's divine and human natures; between ends and means, between life and the meaning of life, between pleasure and the idolization of pleasure, etc. All this leads to war, both within man and, of necessity, between men; a war of thoughts which can lead to real conflicts.

380a

Confusion over the role of morality in regard to power has led to the moral authorities' betrayal of man: instead of bringing leaders and the masses toward God, God has been sought *among* leaders and among the masses, perhaps even amid this power struggle.

380b

The betrayal (on the part of technocratic leaders who super-govern the world) of the naïve, unprepared and bored "citizens of the world," who call themselves such only because they can speak English and have made several transatlantic trips, has happened through confusing the concept of homogenization in the global context, which seeks enrichment born from the fusion of many cultures, civilizations, races, etc. Instead of bringing less evolved cultures up to the level of those that are more "civilized," the opposite has happened, with the more civilized being brought down to the level of the less civilized.

An example of this regards moral laws, which are now imposed by super-governments (European, UN, etc.) in the name of human dignity, or so they say. We have discovered that Gresham's economic law (which explains that bad money drives out good) also applies to morals, with bad morals driving out the good ones—everywhere.

381

It is ever more obvious that the current (2007) economic recession is due to new, global and previously unknown (accelerated delocalization) phenomena, which traditional criteria cannot manage. This consideration makes it doubtful that adequate solutions can be reached quickly and instead prompts us to imagine changes, perhaps even cultural, in the global economic equilibrium. The current crisis is not comparable to any previous crisis. It originated and unfolded in such varying contexts (the USA and Europe, within Europe, within developing countries…); it is on such a global scale that it highlights the inability of individual states, even the largest and most powerful, to fight it off. Yet each political candidate (especially the technocratic ones) claims to have the solution to everything.…

382

We have defined the phenomena that caused this "new and unknown" recession because we are experiencing for the first time a truly global dynamic. Let us consider the "cost inflation" of raw materials (especially petroleum) compensated by a "low consumption deflation." Since the end of the Cold War, first and foremost the USA and Europe have progressively favored the development of the Asiatic area, transferring to that area a great deal of low-cost production aimed at reducing production costs and controlling inflation. Thanks to this, Asia (especially China) has grown too much and too quickly, creating an enormous demand for raw materials in all markets and a high rate of liquidity (which ended up even financing U.S. debt), all the while operating with strategies independent of the Western world. Who knows how these phenomena can be managed?

383

In order to "deflate" the excessive debt produced in the Western world to sustain consumer growth, (in 2008) four ways were thought of. The first was bankruptcy, or not paying the debt: it was considered slightly excessive and undemocratic. The second was inflation, which is a well-tested system of cheating creditors; but the creditors disagreed with this. The third was to search for new "bubbles" to compensate for the losses from the debt, but it was not easy to find bubbles of any description. The fourth was austerity: this was immediately disregarded, as it was unsuitable for a system which had split the world in two: the consumers of the West and the producers of the East, who also had the West's public debt on their hands. Austerity, it was said, would have impeded the economic model, even though with it the West would have gone back to having a greater detachment from material goods, making them reflect on other values.…

384

A possible stable fall in consumption will be able to curb the inflation seen in the costs of raw materials, as demand will fall (cars will not be bought, people will not travel, gas will not be bought...). I would venture to say that the price of gas could return to less than $1.00 [a gallon], if the dollar rises slightly. The negative surprise could come from the difficulty the USA has in containing its deficit (which has risen from 2% to 5% of the GNP), which would be financed by raising interest rates, which would have a worldwide effect and compromise recovery.

385

The "political" lesson to learn is that in these conditions no country can solve its problems on its own; at most it can use "protectionist" policies and pay the consequences. Who would know how to, and could, "solve a problem" like this? If the problems are global and require global solutions, interlocutors with the authority to solve them are needed. The USA has devalued the dollar, aggravating the rise in oil prices and thus transferring many economic problems to Europe, but in Europe who would decide—if it were judged suitable—to devalue the euro?

386a

Another lesson to be learned is that China, Asia and other "emerging countries" are no longer "controllable" and can only be involved in global projects which would make them accept market rules on the one hand (for the purchase of raw materials), and on the other hand accept commercial rules (bringing commercial dumping to an end and making them respect product quality regulations). These countries would have to understand that the survival of the market they find themselves in is at stake, but who could be the European interlocutor, if necessary alongside the USA, with these countries?

386b

The economic crisis "exploded" in 2008, but it was caused in the 1970s thanks to socio-economic policies against nature. It changed almost all the classical economic rules. It changed price mechanisms with exportation of labor. Thanks to this exportation and the advent of new productive systems (as in China) it has changed almost all the laws of supply and demand. It has changed the distribution of income and its very creation. It has changed the nature of work and industrial relations. It has changed governments' economic functions (spending, financing, taxes…). It has changed the logic of savings, consumption and investing. It has changed the nature of monetary exchange and central banks' monetary policies. It has changed the concept of utility and economic value. It has changed the significance of competition, salaries, capital remuneration, profit, development and economic growth. How will all these changes be managed, and by whom? What impact will they have on man? (Above all, who is thinking about these problems?)

387

We can do little by ourselves to resolve the problem of recession. We can restore trust in the market by regulating it better, ensuring that the rules are applied, and restricting speculation. The moral lesson is that once again the tools of the market and of technology have slipped from the grasp of the bankers and technologists. John Paul II foresaw this, and who knows if the lesson will be learned. Let us place this under his protection.

388

The management of a common currency requires a common economic policy, but this involves finding solutions to complex prerequisites, because values must be held in common before anything else. The economy is just an instrument in man's hands. Its use produces moral effects, just as moral considerations inspire economic choices. It is unthinkable to do something for man if an instrument, such as the economy or a currency, becomes an end, and man becomes the means subject to these. It is complicated to make man return to being the end and the economy the means if there is no agreement on what man is and what the meaning of his life is. The economic government of Europe can use a common currency, but if there is no agreement on "why," it will be difficult to agree on "how" to use this means.

389

It is vital to reflect on the fact that man must not only be satisfied materially and intellectually, but also spiritually. If man has a soul, a government takes a great risk and is inexorably headed for failure if it does not consider this fact. The confusion produced by concepts of brotherhood, equality, charity and freedom and the consequent imbalances produced in Europe make a reflection of this type necessary. The old common faith meant there was a unified vision of important things: from what man is, to what is valuable, to what is useful. For centuries Europe inspired the world with these values, because Europe used to produce ideas and men who made them credible.

390

The capacity to produce ideas for the good of man must return to the fore in order to reestablish trust. Trust is based above all on the will to do the common good and the capacity to organize the necessary leadership to accomplish this. This happens because people believe in something superior which orients their life and choices, because they live the values they pursue, and do not just preach them, and the coherent meaning of their actions gives their life some meaning. In the past, faith gave man a common ideal. The rupture in religious unity produced a collapse in these common criteria, promoting two separate and hostile forms of belief, and then a progressive irreligiousness. The common faith was ruptured and led to division of common thought, objectives and will, eventually being substituted with human reason which was not attracted by Heaven, but by atheistic materialism and anarchy. This religious separation broke up a pacifying and unifying influence, and this was especially seen in France, Germany, Italy and Spain. In practice, European countries took different paths with different objectives and different means, preparing themselves for different conflicts, right up till today.

391

Think about what it means to propose a European political and economic program involving religious reunification: people would think you were crazy. This is because the separation was founded on objective reasons, but especially because today there are no bases for reforming the common religious spirit. In time much, or nearly all, of faith and culture has been lost; all has been overtaken, cancelled out and even ridiculed, but worst of all, man himself, a creature, has become the creator, alas....

Now we have a common currency and we wish to establish a common European government. In order to do this we can also unify laws and customs, but to the worst common denominator, since history teaches us that "a bad law drives out a good law." There are questions that need answers: can a civilization construct something stable and sustainable without making their reference values the same? Can the nihilism dominant in these cultures allow man to take back control of the instruments that have taken on moral autonomy? When things go wrong and it is hard to correct the errors; are we sure that it is the instruments that have to be changed, and not the men who use them? How can we change men? The law of stability, the euro, and the European Union—there need to be answers to the above questions in order for any of these to function. All the answers are in *Caritas in Veritate*: have we looked for them, found them and made them our own?

392

Is there an economics of faith? I will give a perhaps surprising and apparently contradictory answer. Earthly life is a constant struggle, sometimes a contradictory one, between what we think we are and what we really are. It is a struggle in which we have to fight against our natural instincts while another voice tells us to follow them, which can be confusing. For me, living the faith means living everyday life with absolute naturalness, but on one condition: that some essential moments are prepared for and planned. This naturalness requires us to be clear about what life is and what our behavior should be in order to live it fully.

I can use a paradox: he who does not live by faith does not live life at all. To explain myself, as I am not a theologian, I will seek at least to be logical. As I said before, living life means having understood and accepted what life is. If I am confused about what life is, it will be hard to live it as I should. To get to the point: living life means always finding the meaning in every moment and context, at work, in the family, in society. If life has no meaning because we are convinced that man is the result of chaos and/or evolution from a cell, it is obvious that the dignity of life, of man himself, is limited, and we are limited to material needs and instincts. In practice, pleasure is taken only in a life filled with purely material (in every sense of the word) satisfaction. From this we feel the satisfactions that intelligent animals (as some claim we are) feel.

If we feel we are children of God, life obviously takes on a very different significance. Man begins to think that if he was created, it was with a specific purpose, and he wants to understand what that purpose is and what he must do in reply. Being convinced that we are children of God is equivalent to an act of faith, but to live out this act of faith, we must discover the meaning of life and of our actions; otherwise we have faith, but we live like an intelligent animal. This is not easy, and reflection and effort are needed to understand what the Creator wants from His creatures, and this effort gives rise to unthinkable grace to totally rational men.

Normally this was taught (and in some places still is) by priests teaching doctrine. Living by faith means living coherently with one's nature as child of God, and valuing one's life as if it were the most important in the world and for the world, after that of Christ. I have no doubt that if we knew how to live our faith we would all be protagonists of redemption; we would be co-redeemers and perform miracles. I believe I have made quite an impression on the reader, but perhaps I have done so by directly injecting these thoughts into the secular mindset of those who are, and feel they are, God's children.

These economics of faith require us to know how to live in God's presence: if you understand what I have written above, what I am about to say will seem elementary. Living in God's presence means speaking to Him constantly. I do not mean as if He were present: if you have faith, He is always present. It is stupid to ask whether He hears us. Not only does He listen to us, but He even wants us to speak to Him, He wants our questions. It is even more ridiculous to ask whether He answers us, but in order to believe, you have to try....

394

In these economics of faith it is necessary to know how to listen to God: remaining in silence after speaking with Him, waiting for His answers, signs, illuminations, even His surprises. God surprises us; His relationship with us is full of surprises. It is useless to think that God only speaks to us if we are worthy: this is useless because we cannot even imagine what it really means to be worthy, but He knows whether we are worthy. I have often had the impression that He was not taking me seriously when I was explaining important things to Him and that He preempted me in deciding what was really important, and it really has been so. I thought of it as a continual attempt, disappointment, attempt and finally getting what I wanted: this was wrong. Getting things wrong is natural for us creatures, but it is not wrong to get things wrong; rather it is wrong to get discouraged and not trust, and it is wrong only to trust in ourselves. No, worse than that, trusting only in ourselves is ridiculous, as it means we are immature and do not know ourselves fully. How can we trust ourselves completely if we know ourselves, if we know our defects, deficiencies, weaknesses, vices and disorders? Maybe we do not know them, and that is even worse. Perhaps we are indulgent, and this is a danger and a weakness. Let us ask ourselves and show whether we can truly mortify our intelligence, our thoughts and convictions, our bodies (and their various appetites), our characters and imaginations. Can we honestly say we have succeeded? No, we haven't—or only very, very rarely—and we claim to be "like God"?

395

The economics of faith helps us to keep a distance from the logic of the world, but to succeed in this we must have understood what the world is and what we are. Going against the tide is in itself neither difficult nor always useful: it is difficult and useful to turn the tide and make it go where it should. This means that instead of keeping one's distance from the logic of the world, it is better to understand it, analyze it and try to influence it. Very often the logic of the world is just a deformation of good logic, and not always the work of the "Evil One." Then, with great humility we should always ask ourselves whether whoever is behind the logic of "this world" is not more credible than whoever proposes the logic of "another world." It is not enough to be certain of what is good to know how to put it forward.

It is strange to note that among the Church's worst enemies are some of her former members, and among her greatest defenders there are some of her former enemies. Faith seems to change man, but man thinks he can change faith. Going back to the logic of this world, I believe it is the dominant culture that is the object of battle. What should be understood is that if ideas cannot influence behavior, behavior will influence ideas. Ideas require continuous education, training and combat for them to become true and strong ideas. I believe that man was created to think, and then to work (*ut operaretur*): how could man work if he could not first think about what work means? Concerning the crisis that makes it difficult to keep a distance from the logic of this world and the consequent behavioral crisis, two self-analytical questions for the reader suffice: are we always able to distinguish between ends and means, and are we certain that in order to reach good ends we must always use equally good means? Let us think about this in relation to concrete situations, and I fear we will be surprised.

396

Do these economics of faith give optimism? Does faith help us to be optimistic, to dream of the big picture? It is hard for me to answer yes, perhaps because by nature (with which I have obviously struggled but little) I am not an optimist, or perhaps because in the world where

I work, the imposed and hard-to-influence mechanisms allow you to feel optimistic only if you see things from afar and do not have adequate evaluation criteria. Therefore, rather than a generic optimism I prefer an appropriate subjective realism, which not only does not undervalue "opposing" forces but also does not undervalue the immense effort that a "saint in the world" must make in order to triumph.

The related problem is that often we do not understand where these opposing forces are, or perhaps they seem to be on our side and we do not understand them. Sometimes they look and speak like their adversaries and confuse their allies. Unfortunately the results can be seen and heard. Perhaps some will think I am exaggerating, but I worry about ignorant optimism, preferring the optimism of those who are certain that *"non prevalebunt"* and prepare themselves well to have an effect in the field where they have decided to bring about improvement and are thus optimistic of success. The optimism of those who hope that others will solve (even their own) problems does not convince me. I would be much more optimistic if we were encouraged, educated and always assisted by many holy priests who spoke about God and eternal life.

397

Thus this economy of faith needs to be shared, so it can truly have an effect on the economy. How can I spread my economy of faith? We know from the teachings of saints and popes that man requires three types of nourishment: corporal, intellectual and spiritual. Leaving aside the corporal, it is the intellectual and spiritual nourishment that sustain a reasonable faith that can operate in the world. In simple terms, this "food" is made up of the Eucharist and study.

I believe that this is objectively common to all who want to be apostles in the world; as far as the spread of faith is concerned, the ways and means are more subjective. In the end, an apostolate is "also or above all" personal; it uses criteria based on different spiritual formations and uses necessary structures of organization, but claiming a soul comes from the relationship between the soul and God through an apostle. This model of apostolate is not the same for all, in my experience. Each person is persuaded in different ways, every person does things with varying degrees of enthusiasm, and different people seek the same aims with different skills and aptitudes. I believe I have skills that let me appeal to people's heads rather than to their emotions or feelings.

I know in fact that our work is always incomplete or insufficient, and to do it better it is necessary to study and train oneself, even in apologetics. A defect in modern candidates for the apostolate is their lack of knowledge of apologetics, indispensable for defending the Church against secular attacks. Today more than ever it is indispensable to know how to appeal to the "head," and this is why training before acting is indispensable. I would like to give an example: how many people would know how to debate on the question of whether truth or liberty comes first? It would be interesting were the reader to put himself to the test.

I wish to conclude with the answer given by our great Pope Benedict XVI in the encyclical *Caritas in Veritate*: nihilism is the enemy to combat. To return to order man must return to feeling he is a child of God and live accordingly. Man, much more than tools, must be changed in order to change the world.

398

How can we explain the economic crisis to a simple country pastor, a man filled with faith and busy about charitable works, who is justly concerned about the drop in his parish's income? I could try by means of a parable—perhaps one inspired by the Old Testament, such as the story of Joseph:

"The pharaoh called Joseph and confided to him his worries and dreams. The dream Joseph interpreted is the following: the pharaoh had dreamed that the Egyptian population growth was so sluggish that it meant a weakening in the offensive and defensive capabilities of his army. He had then dreamed that, thanks to the forced immigration of too many slaves over the last few years, the slaves had become as numerous as the Egyptians and were now a threat. Not only that, but he had also dreamed that wars with neighboring countries would be on the rise, depriving the countryside of labor, so the harvests and stores of grain would dwindle more quickly than estimated, and there would be a famine.

"Joseph suggested that he make peace with the neighboring countries to avoid wasting men and resources. Then he suggested building fewer pyramids and more houses for the Egyptian population, and after that freeing the slaves, but above all, encouraging a rise in the birthrate in order to increase his nation's power and wealth.

"The pharaoh continued to dream of being attacked by millions of starving people, but now, irritated by Joseph's suggestions, he decided to interpret the dream himself. He concluded that the starving masses were due to an excessively high birthrate, so he decreed that for the following twenty years no children should be born. He obliged the women, who would no longer be carrying children, to increase the grain harvest.

"He then declared five wars simultaneously, counting on winning them all and dividing the spoils with the Egyptian people, to assuage them materially in compensation for not having children and for the women having to work.

"But wars are expensive, and the children not being born meant fewer soldiers, and the elderly neither fight in wars nor gather grain. Thus Egypt's costs rose, the harvests decreased, and the soldiers died; and when they lost wars, wealth was lost as well, so the hungry and tired population began to worry the pharaoh. He then decided, in order to keep them happy, to have a pyramid built for each Egyptian family, financing them with fifty-year mortgages, borrowing money in turn from his neighbors.

"But having pyramids did not allow Egyptian families to produce sufficient wealth to pay them off, so the Egyptians did not pay their mortgages, and the pharaoh in turn did not pay off his neighbors, who got angry and declared war on him. Their fighters were younger (as they had continued having children) and were neither slaves nor mercenaries, so they won the war, subjugated the Egyptian people and replaced the pharaoh.

"The pharaoh now had Joseph reinterpret his dream and saw that earlier he himself had misinterpreted it. The millions of starving people who had attacked him were not newborns but angry Egyptian adults. By then it was too late, as the pharaoh's civilization was

finished, and Joseph in turn was unemployed and disappointed that
he had been unable to convince the pharaoh that dreams, just like
economic well-being, harvests, pyramids, loans and wars, must be
interpreted correctly, without bluffing or cheating, but above all that
the dearth of children cannot be made up for with pyramids or
slaves."

399

That's how it went, dear Reverend. About thirty years ago the
Egyptians of the twentieth century decided that the earth was unable
to support the previous birth rate, and that if things were to continue
that way, then millions would die of hunger. These Egyptians of the
twentieth century had many wars going on, and thus many costs to
bear. They discovered that if the population does not increase
sufficiently, then fixed costs (pensions and health costs of an aging
population) increase, and so do taxes. Savings and financial
transactions diminish and economic growth is blocked.

Non-existent or low economic growth always worries a
government and its pharaoh-president, because they do not want to
do without their wars or sending rockets to the moon. The Egyptians
of the twentieth century sought to increase the population through
immigration, but this was not enough to fill the gap, so they decided
to create rapid growth by increasing consumption, to compensate for
the lack of population growth. They transferred production to low-
cost countries (China, India), bringing the finished goods back at
lower costs; they created the *net economy* (which immediately failed)
and then began offering home loans to risky sectors of the population
(*subprime* mortgages). To compensate for the lack of savings, having
forced families into debt first through consumption and then through
their home purchases, they invented a nice substitute, *derivatives*—and
we all know how that ended!

400

In the twentieth century there are pharaohs who dream of
catastrophes and draw up anti-catastrophe plans which cause
disasters. The Josephs ready to interpret these dreams and make

suggestions have existed, and still do, but since their suggestions include moral teachings, they are ignored. Economics has gained its moral autonomy from religion, hasn't it?

Exactly.